DIGITAL LIBRARIES
IN
HIGHER EDUCATION

DIGITAL LIBRARIES IN HIGHER EDUCATION

By
Dr. Amjad Ali
Deputy Librarian
Aligarh Muslim University, Aligarh

Ess Ess Publications

4837/24, Ansari Road, Darya Ganj,
New Delhi-110002
✆ : 23260807
Fax : 23274173
E-mail: info@essessreference.com
url:http://www.essessreference.com

First Published 2005

ISBN : 81-7000-429-2

Price : Rs. 550/-

Published by :

Ess Ess Publications

4837/24, Ansari Road, Darya Ganj,
New Delhi - 110 002
Phone : 23260807
Fax : 23274173
E-mail: info@essessreference.com
url:http://www.essessreference.com

Laser Typesetting:

Mukesh Graphics

T-1264, Mangolpuri, New Delhi
Ph. : 0-9818192305
E-mail:mukeshgraphics29@hotmail.com

Printed at :

Print Line

Contents

Dedicated to My
MOTHER

PREFACE

Digital technologies are making inroads into the system of education all over the world bringing information and education closer and closer day by day. As a result, more and more educational institutions are being transformed into virtual campuses. Digital libraries are emerging as substitute to the traditional libraries with enhanced facilities at a lower cost. It may be said that the infrastructure does not exist suitably to be benefited equally at present but a precedent may be taken of the expansion of computer in the same conditions. Once developed and connected, the digital libraries will supercede all the traditional libraries of today reducing them to merely the museum of books.

The digital libraries promise to provide many social, economic, scholarly, and technical advantages to the information based activities in higher education enabling access and manipulation of information over networked environments and providing enhanced services to the clients. But there are still many issues to be addressed to by them.

This book presents a brief account of the changing international scenario of higher education as a result of the technological innovations and the digitization projects undertaken by the libraries of some selected universities of USA, UK, Australia and India. It also addresses to the problems and prospects of digital libraries for the institutions of higher education.

An attempt has been made to provide information on the development of digital libraries in varied situations. Some of the libraries covered in the book have acquired maturity in their design and functioning whereas the others are still at the stage of infancy. Although the formats of the various chapters contained in the book lack uniformity yet the details of their activities have been presented in a way to give an insight into their needs, functions, design and development which will be useful for the institutions who have an agenda to digitize their library resources.

I am indebted to a number of individuals and institutions who have contributed their information resources to the World Wide Web on the subject of digital libraries and higher education which I referred to bring out this volume. M/S Ess Ess Publications, New Delhi also deserve my thanks for bringing out this book in a very short time after submission of the manuscript.

It is hoped that the book will be useful for the students and faculty of library and information science, working librarians and information professionals, educationists and all those persons who are interested in recording, retrieval and utilization of information through the modern means.

Dr. Amjad Ali

Email: *amjad_alig@yahoo.co.in*

1
The Higher Education Scenario

Higher education is being imparted in the society by universities since long. The term university originated from the Latin word universitas which means an organized body of individuals or a corporation. In the past, there was no fixed place for study of individuals and universitas meant a fraternity of scholars. The term did not indicate the concept of universality, a term which is considered today to be fundamental to the idea of a university.

The forerunner of modern higher education in Europe was a medical school at Salerno in Southern Italy which was established in the 9th century AD. Later, institutions were established as centres for traveling teachers and scholars and their main objective was to propagate the intellectual events of the time.

Modern form of universities existed for over a millennium. The Oxford University and the University of Paris are some 800 years old, making them amongst the oldest institutions of any type still surviving (and still flourishing) today. The origins of universities even predate these ancient institutions, being able to be traced back to an institution established by Plato in ancient Greece and to the colleges to train government administrators in ancient China.

The universities took their defined form in the recent past. A century ago universities developed all over the world according to British models, functioned as, what one observer described as 'finishing schools for gentlemen', serving only men from the elite social class and preparing them for leadership roles in a very conservative and structured society. The 'ivory tower' image of universities – which saw universities as being remote from society – was very much in evidence.

The Second World War experience proved the value of science and technology to economic development and formed the basis for post-war industrialization. Research, knowledge generation and innovation became synonymous with the modernisation. Universities were recognised as being able to contribute significantly to this movement. Universities were also used to retrain ex-servicemen and women for civilian jobs. At the same time higher education became seen as a prerequisite for an increasing range of professions. The rigid social class system broke down and in the good economic times of the 1950s and '60s more people wanted to access a university education as a means of social and vocational advancement. From 1950-75 more universities were built and a system of colleges of advanced education was established to provide ever-increasing higher education opportunities to an increasingly diverse cross-section of society.

The expansion in the university system since the Second World War has been dramatic. During the process of expansion, the university sector has changed from being an elite to a mass education system. Where once the student body drew from a narrow elite segment of society, universities now serve all of society. Where once universities provided what was referred to as a 'general liberal education' and were involved in training in only the more elite vocations such as medicine and law, universities now prepare graduates for work in a wide variety of vocations from business, teaching and nursing to tourism/hospitality and journalism.

With the explosion in knowledge that has now occurred in the age of computers, information technology and the Internet, universities are even more important for job training. People now need to enroll in universities for retraining, as knowledge and skills become redundant at ever-increasing rates. 'Lifelong learning' is now the norm.

Now, success at university primarily depends on how well students understand the culture of the university and on how well they can navigate their way through university processes. To enhance chances of success at university, it is important to understand the history of universities and the nature of university culture. Academic work is based around critical inquiry. One should take the initiative to study the work thoroughly and take pains to seek out references and other relevant materials beyond the set recommended reading to further support work and provide with extended insights into course of study.

The fundamental product of universities is knowledge. Universities function on the basis of innate curiosity–seeking knowledge on issues regardless of whether that knowledge has any clear practical application or use. Although often criticized as impractical, this trait is actually the basis for most real innovation as important disciplines such as computer science, biotechnology and nuclear physics all arose from 'pure' research for which practical applications were not obvious when that research was commenced.

Now, scholars typically specialise in a particular area of knowledge – which can sometimes be particularly narrow indeed – for example, becoming a specialist in the wing structure of a particular species of fly. Scholars are often described as 'people who know a lot about a little'. This depth of knowledge is necessary to position scholars to add new knowledge to their own area of expertise and forms the basis for humanity moving ever forward in its understanding of things.

Advances in academic disciplines occur through people putting forward different opinions or theories to explain things and then seeing which holds up best. This process is called 'disputation'. If someone has a point of view that differs from someone else's they are encouraged to put it forward as long as it is supported with good arguments or evidence. Theories are constantly being introduced, amended and mixed together

– this is how our overall understanding of things improves.

Universities rely on the free flow of ideas and continuous debate. Ideas will stand or fall on the strength of the arguments and evidence that support them, but there must always be opportunities for existing ideas to be challenged and for different points of view to be put forward. This should occur in a constructive way, never maliciously.

Scholars are as critical of their own ideas as they are about the ideas of others. Scholars need to be cautious about making statements unless there is good evidence to support them. In academic life it is seen as preferable to live with uncertainty – to admit that they 'just don't know' – unless there is compelling evidence to support a particular point of view. The aim of academic writing is to seek the truth through logical and ordered processes, not just to try and put together 'a good story'.

The essential core of any university is its staff and students who interact, engage in dialogue and debate, and generally create a productive and creative academic environment. The way that staff members interact with each other and with students is critical to maintaining an effective academic environment. Universities operate on democratic principles and 'collegiality' describes the arrangement whereby staff and students treat each other fairly and with respect as a professional collective.

Internationalization

Universities have been greatly affected by the internationalization of other services like telecommunication, and transportation. An international culture is in the offing for everyone who has exposure to these developments.

Each year, the world gets smaller. Multinational corporations provide more and more goods and services that are recognizable on every continent. The economy in one region affects the others. Jobs move quickly from one nation to another. Environmental and public health issues have no boundaries. Education itself is being viewed as a commodity that can be exported or imported to meet social, political and economic demands. The old distinctions of national, domestic, foreign are blurring. Most refer to this as the "globalization" of the 21st century societies.

Higher education is just becoming aware of the ramifications of this "new world." As in every sea change which tends to define eras of history, there are some who arrive first to explore the implications of the shift in paradigms. Surely we would hope that educators are among those who have both the curiosity and the courage to study these major shifts and to prepare students to live and work in new environments. Indeed, many within the academy have been promoting the internationalization of higher learning for several decades. Now the topic is center stage.

Every external indicator points to the need for higher education to become more international in its thinking, its students, its faculty and its curriculum. This is not a singular program, but a long-term "over lay" on what a campus does. This will require leadership at the top. We can all start with small steps that will, almost by themselves, draw others into more expanded efforts. Each country and each campus will be unique, but can learn much from the experience of others. The consequences for world peace and human development are real. And very much worth the effort.

In spite of resistance to change, we must be ready to take advantage of world, or national, or campus events, to make progress incrementally. In America, World War II probably marked the point at which large numbers of people saw the need to be more aware of other parts of the world. National security was a key motivator. So governments started investing money in graduate students' study abroad. The Fulbright Program, alone, has assisted over 200,000 Americans to study in over 130 nations since 1942. The American government has also invested in research centers which focus on specific issues or areas of the world. The Cold War sustained the impetus for more study of certain cultures. All these efforts led naturally to conferences, papers, more research, visitors from universities in other countries. Slowly, momentum built for more of the same but also for expanding opportunities to others.

Other governments are creating similar initiatives. The UK is marketing its educational assets around the world. Germany, France and Australia are among other nations where the national government has set goals, provided funding, and given direction to encourage local campuses.

On a particular campus, normally it is just a few faculty or administrators who begin to champion internationalization. Often this begins by encouraging students to study for part of their education in another land. The 250,000 students who study abroad each year often return as the catalysts for change. More of the 500,000 foreign students on our campuses will offer to help internationalize the campus by sharing more of their culture in both curricular and extra-curricular settings. Faculty who have studied or simply traveled abroad frequently bring more international flavor into their lectures and reading assignments. Many small efforts lead to campus-wide change. We must be comfortable with incremental change. And each of us can make a contribution.

While change will be incremental, we must also be prepared to make the case for more systematic strategic planning. There are many sources of knowledge and experience from which to learn.

National governments should help provide leadership through general policies and priorities. Many governments have already done so and provide funding for those strategies which are important to political leaders. In every culture, the availability of outside funding promotes change!

Next, professional societies, associations of universities of which there are several hundred, foundations which give grant money or sponsor programs themselves, mass media, research organizations, even well-known individual scholars - all of these have a role to play. They can often promote ideas that catch on with enough people that universities see the need to be responsive.

Change on a campus usually requires the top leadership to show more than casual interest. Internationalization needs to be a stated priority by the top administrative and academic leaders. That gives permission, and often releases some funding, for educationists to begin taking this issue seriously.

This diversity among institutions is carried further by the wide variety of programs within any given institution. At the campus level, any strategy must be consistent with the mission and values of the campus. The common faith of the public all over the world gives the campuses a natural incentive to be more international. Yet, there is great diversity in the particular strategies which such campuses might choose to be more global.

In the Chinese system of higher education, and in most nations where the central government plays the leading role in education policy, more direction will come from those leaders. But at some level, each campus must design plans within those broader policy guidelines. In most nations, individual campuses will, for many different reasons, focus on different aspects of their internationalization strategy.

Scholars of every country associated with higher education like to document, compare, evaluate and publish. They should find it easier and easier to learn from one another and discover strategies that work best in certain situations. They should participate with those who started earlier. That is what is seen happening with the internationalization of higher learning in most of the countries.

Some Challenges

There are many people living all over the world, specially in America who believe that campuses should move quickly to embrace more people of the other faith, particularly those from the Middle East. But the grief remains over the risk involved to them and some people are not yet ready to give "equal time". Unfortunately, bias for our own and prejudice against others is part of the human condition. Yet, the people in higher education can recognize these obstacles while still believing that learning is a necessary ingredient to overcoming them. It is often education that brings hope to the poor, opportunity to the disadvantaged, access to a better life for the oppressed, reasons to pursue peace. This high purpose for education keeps us going in spite of the obstacles. Learning from others is easier today, but it is always a challenge to translate knowledge into wisdom for our own educational practices. There is great opportunity to waste time and money if we do not move thoughtfully..

There is a serious problem of funding in higher education that will always be a challenge. We can want to do something right, but simply can not afford it. So we need to be "making the case" to funding organizations. Government agencies, multi-national corporations, large foundations, wealthy individuals from many nations - all of these need to hear our plans and interests and be convinced of the need to invest in strategic programs to help advance peace through learning in the 21st century.

Globalization in India

The phenomenon of globalization, which transformed world trade, communications and economic relations in the latter part of the 20th Century, is having a similarly profound effect on education at the start of the 21st century. Student options for higher education, in particular, are no longer constrained by national boundaries. Innovative forms of transnational education - Internet-based distance learning, branch campuses and educational "franchising" have greatly expanded opportunities for students to study and learn outside their country of origin. In addition, there is now increasing global competition for the "best and brightest" students, as more and more countries recognize the economic potential of higher education as a service export sector. For the first time in history, large segments of the world's student population truly have access to a "global marketplace" of higher education.

The new environment of higher education in India, holds both threats and opportunities. The threats are obvious: as more and more Indian students look to Australia, Britain and the U.S. for both undergraduate and post-graduate studies, the quality of Indian universities will continue to suffer. Lacking computer facilities and Internet access, many of India's resource-starved institutions will be on the wrong side of the "digital divide." Even India's elite institutions - the IITs and IIMs will find it increasingly difficult to attract and retain world class faculty members in the face of attractive offers from foreign universities, research institutes and multi-national corporations. So, there is a substantial risk that Indian universities and their students could end up as serious losers in the global higher education "game".

There are also real opportunities too for India to benefit significantly from the global revolution in higher education. To do so will require major policy reforms in the way Indian universities are structured, funded and regulated. It will also require closer links between Indian industry, especially the growing technology-based sector, and Indian universities. And, it will require a new, globally oriented, entrepreneurial style of leadership by Indian Vice Chancellors and other top-level administrators. With these ingredients, India has the potential to capture the "up-side" benefits of globalization, emerging with a stronger, better, more globally competitive higher education system, and greater opportunities for Indian students.

The question to be discussed here is that which path will India take? There are certain to be differences of opinion about the mixed blessings of globalization among leading Indian educators and policymakers. Some pathways for it are suggested by which India can achieve tangible gains from current global trends in higher education, without sacrificing its national goals for higher education development or abandoning its commitment to Indian cultural values.

In the Indian higher education institutions today, the legacy of prior waves of international, if not global, influence can be seen in virtually every field. The impact of British higher education is felt not only in the basic structure of Indian higher education - the system of examinations, structure of post-secondary education, scheme of universities and affiliating colleges - but also in the range of colonial era institutions that are still among the most elite in India today. St. Stephens College in Delhi and Presidency College, Calcutta, are but two examples of prestigious undergraduate institutions that still bear the distinct imprint of their British heritage.

Similarly, India hosts a wide variety of pre-Independence missionary institutions and colleges founded in the late 19th and early 20th Centuries by foreign missionaries of different faiths. St. Joseph's College in Trichy, St. Xavier's in Chennai, and Christian Medical College, Vellore, are notable examples. Some of these, such as CMC Vellore (founded in 1900 by a Cornell-trained American woman physician to train women nurses and doctors) and Isabella Thoburn College (founded by an American social worker to provide educational opportunities for young women in Lucknow), intertwined social reform agendas with their religious philosophies.

In the post-Independence era, the Indian Institutes of Technology, consciously patterned after the Massachusetts Institute of Technology in the U.S., received substantial overseas help right from the outset. With support from four donor nations, the five IITs benefited from guest faculty from outside of India, the ability to send Indian faculty for training abroad, and contributions of modern laboratory equipment and facilities. Similar international links were established by the Indian Institutes of Management: IIM/Ahmenabad, for example, still maintains strong connections with the Harvard Business School. Perhaps the most recent innovation in Indian higher education, the Indira Gandhi National Open University (together with similar, state-sponsored Open Universities), drew heavily on the UK experience with distance education and the Open University concept.

Even the most genuinely "Indian" of Indian institutions, Santiniketan, kept its windows wide open to international ideas, influences and experience. Conceived by its founder, Rabindrinath Tagore, as an international center for humanistic and cultural studies, Santiniketan captured the ancient Sanskrit notion of a "world in one nest." In inaugurating Visva-Bharati in 1921, Tagore spoke of India's "wealth of mind which is for all." In creating a center where East meets West, Tagore acknowledged both "India's obligation to offer to others the hospitality of her best culture and India's right to accept from others their best."

The Global Marketplace

As per the statistics available, of the 514,000 foreign students currently studying in the United States, more than 54 percent are from Asia. Seven of the top ten "sending countries" of international foreign students in the U.S. are Asian, while not a single Asian country is represented among the top ten destinations for American students studying abroad. India alone accounts for more than 42,000 students in the U.S., compared to only 707 Americans who studied in India during the 1998/99 academic year. The current data about their enrolment reveals that 15,000 Indians have got admission in the universities of United Kingdom in the year 2004. Worldwide student mobility data, compiled annually by UNESCO confirm similar imbalances in student exchange between India and other industrialized countries.

The liberalization of the Indian economy, a process that began in 1991, is certainly a major factor behind the large and growing numbers of Indian students seeking education abroad. Prior to the 1990s, only a privileged few Indian families could afford to send their children to universities outside of

India. With the dramatic rise of a new Indian middle class (and increased wealth of the Indian upper class), the numbers of students able to pursue foreign education has skyrocketed. For example, the number of Indian students studying in the U.S. grew by more than 46 percent from 1990 to 1999.

In contrast to many other Asian students surveyed recently by EduWorld, an Australian research firm, Indian students were not forced to look outside of their home country to find their desired course of study, at least at the undergraduate level. Instead, the quality of education and the perceived value of an overseas degree appear to be the most significant factors influencing student decisions to study outside of India. It is also noteworthy that, for more than one-third of such students, a major motivation was their desire to broaden their experience by living and working in another country.

While the in-country availability of desired courses at the undergraduate level may not be a major factor in the student mobility equation, the limited capacity of India's institutions to meet the demand for post-graduate education in particular fields may be a more serious problem. More than 70 percent of Indian students studying in the U.S. are pursuing post-graduate degrees; only 22 percent are undergraduate students. Business/management, engineering, math and computer sciences account for more than 75 percent of all Indian students in the U.S.

It is also well known that the demand for "seats" at India's apex institutions for Indian students in highly competitive fields such as engineering and management vastly exceeds the supply. Reservation policies, designed to ensure educational opportunities for disadvantaged groups within Indian society, further limit the in-country slots available for students from forward caste backgrounds. To a certain extent then, foreign universities provide a safety valve for talented, well-off Indian students who cannot find seats in their chosen fields within Indian institutions.

A final factor worth noting is the active and growing competition for the best Indian students among foreign universities. While the UK and (more recently) the USA are well-established destinations for Indian students, Australia and Canada are rapidly gaining in "market share". In recent years, Australia, the UK and France have all launched aggressive student outreach/recruitment efforts in Asia. Stung by declining enrollments from East and Southeast Asian countries affected by the Asian currency crisis of the late 1990s, American universities have also intensified their marketing efforts to students in South Asia.

While all of these factors help explain the large number of Indian students studying outside their home country, what accounts for the small number of foreign students studying in India? In large measure, the answer lies in some of the same factors motivating Indian student to study overseas i.e., the lower perceived quality and "marketability" of qualifications from Indian institutions. But other, more easily controlled factors also play a role. Significant among these is the relative paucity of structured and accredited college "study abroad" programs for foreign students in India.

The Institute of International Education annually publishes a directory of study abroad programs for U.S. students seeking a semester or academic year of study in another country. The 2000/2001 edition of IIE's Academic Year Abroad directory lists just 21 such programs for American students in India. This number compares with 242 programs in France, 214 in Australia, 97 in Japan and 26 in Thailand. Given the wide availability of English-medium courses in India, the subcontinent's rich cultural, historical and ecological resources, and its well-developed higher education infrastructure, India should be a much more popular destination for Western students than it currently is. There is clearly a large, untapped potential to attract increased numbers of foreign students to experience India's "wealth of mind."

The Indian higher education system comprises of over 300 universities and deemed universities, more than 10,000 colleges and some 6.5 million students. Massification of higher education has overwhelmed large parts of this system, resource constraints are severe, and the quality of education available to most Indian students has deteriorated markedly in recent years. The situation is further complicated by the rigidities of India's centralized higher education bureaucracy, the political pressures on higher education institutions from regional, religious and caste-based groups, and the growing problem of corruption in various aspects of university life. In such a beleaguered system, internationalization efforts are bound to suffer seriously.

There is some hope and promise for the future. While system-wide higher education reform may not be feasible politically, a targeted and incremental approach to liberalization of higher education is essential in order for India to take advantage of opportunities in the new global environment. Making educational exchange a more central feature of Indian foreign policy could also produce tangible benefits for India's relations with other countries and for Indian universities and students.

A second pathway for Indian internationalists has to do with partnerships. In fields such as engineering, management and computer sciences, for example, industry-university collaborations can yield significant benefits for both sides. The growing presence of multi-national corporations in India, together with India's own emerging high tech industry, holds considerable promise for university partnerships in areas such as curriculum development, equipment donations, faculty training and student scholarships. Global companies such as General Electric and Lucent Technologies have already shown an interest and willingness to support international education initiatives, such as scholarship programs for highly talented Indian students. They join a long list of Indian firms and industrial houses that have seen higher education as a worthwhile investment for both practical and philanthropic reasons.

Stronger partnerships also need to be developed between Indian universities and universities in other countries. In Thailand, IIE has worked with the Ministry of University Affairs to develop an internet-based "matchmaking service" for Thai and U.S. universities interested in developing linkage projects. Project JUNO (Joint Universities Network Online) enables Thai universities to explore potential opportunities for student or faculty exchanges, develop joint courses, and undertake collaborative research with interested U.S. counterparts. A similar service could easily be developed for Indian universities, and could open up new avenues for Indo-U.S. educational linkages and collaboration.

A more systematic focus on institutional partnerships could also become part of India's approach to bi-lateral scholarly exchange programs, such as those sponsored by Fulbright, DAAD, and the British Council. In order to achieve a wider institutional "ripple effect" from individual Fulbright senior scholar exchanges, the U.S. State Department and IIE's Council for International Exchange of Scholars this year established a new Alumni Initiatives Awards program. This program supports collaborative follow-on activities between the home and host universities of recently returned American Fulbright scholars. A relatively modest investment in similar follow-on projects for returned Indian Fulbrighters could help sustain linkages and networks between their home institutions and the universities where they studied or taught while abroad.

Innovation and leadership are two qualities in greatest need within Indian higher education today. Innovation can take a variety of forms, ranging from the use of internet technology to develop joint on-line courses between Indian and foreign universities to institutional innovations like the recent initiative by SNDT Women's University to establish an overseas branch campus for women students in the Gulf region. Successful innovation does not take place without leadership, however. The Institute of Rural Management, Anand, would never have come into existence without the personal commitment of its "champion," NDDB Chairman Dr. V. Kurien. The National Law School University of India would not be the premier institution it is today without the leadership of its founding director, Professor Madhava Menon. Wherever one finds excellence and innovation taking place in higher education today, it is directly connected to the efforts of a dynamic, energetic and committed leader or group of leaders. For India to broaden and expand its niche in the global marketplace of higher education will require bold and innovative leadership by university vice chancellors, political leaders, administrators and policymakers at the central and state levels.

The world of higher education in the 21st century can truly be a border-less world of knowledge and ideas which will yield reciprocal benefits for all nations. There is no single, simple path for reaching this new global future, but instead, multiple pathways that lead toward "a world in one nest." Detractors of global higher education raise the specter of Western universities dominating the educational landscape in the way that McDonalds has come to dominate the global fast food industry. With foresight, skill and determination, today's leaders of Indian universities have it within their power to craft a different kind of globalization, one which affirms and values cultural difference and encourages greater mobility for all students.

2
IT in Higher Education

After the invention of printing press and computer. Internet is the next paradigm shift in human life. It has provided a powerful medium of communication for individuals of different tastes. And education is no exception. Virtual universities are being established all over the world and the beginning has already been made in India with about all major cities organizing such institutional support to the students. One can enroll with such universities for the desired academic course without being physically present.

With increasing convergence between computer and communication technologies and the spread of telecommunication networks, present day universities are expected to gradually transform themselves as virtual universities where all functions of the university will take place electronically over the digital links and networks,

During the last two decades, the importance of non-book materials as carriers of information has got a wider recognition along with the technical aids to retrieve information from them. It started with the availability of duplication techniques and later with the recording and reproduction of sight and sound.

It is often said that a picture is worth a thousand words as it may communicate a huge mass of ideas, which may mean differently to different people. Photography emerged as an appropriate medium for such presentation, which coupled with the technology of sound proved to be the greatest and the most significant form for presentation of ideas.

Audiovisuals

The present day photography is the result of the early observations by alchemists and chemists based on the action of light on the photosensitive materials. The technique developed towards the end of the 18th century when the demand for the pictures grew. A major advancement in photography took place with substitution f glass for paper as a carrier for the light sensitive material. In 1851, once the manufacture of photographic materials was established as a commercial industry, the photographic techniques followed steady growth. In 1912 Kodak Company introduced flat film in place of glass plates for making negatives. The technique was advantageous for manufacturers. A few years later, the development in new sensitizing dyes made it possible for preparing panchromatic materials of improved quality.

Photography coupled with sound heralded a new era in field of communication of ideas. It followed the invention and application of a variety of technologies for recording and presentation of information. It began with the art of sight and sound which later transformed into tape slide shows. But with further improvements in synchronization of sound with the moving images, the present day cinematography took its birth.

The development in photography and cinematography brought significant changes in the world of learning. Now more sense organs were involved in the perception process. The human nature is so that the maximum of ones total knowledge is perceived through the senses of sight and sound and the new media of communication available as a result of these advancements exploited this potential of man to its fall, facilitating learning at a higher speed and with a greater ease. The trend was on for about thirty years in India from the mid of the last century. The celluloid medium was primarily adopted for entertainment but soon it became equally popular in the academic circles. Film became the medium of instruction within fifty years of its existence.

Motion Pictures

Motion pictures are now available on cinematographic film as well as on video. Their basic and common characteristic is the movement of picture on the screen. The movement is achieved by running a film or video through a projector or player at a speed of 24 frames per second. The stills are recorded in a situation where all of them are comparatively similar and differ only at the point where movement has to be visualized. Motion pictures include silent and sound films as well. Nowadays, nearly all of them are being recorded in color.

Motion pictures are being accepted increasingly by the academic circles as a learning aid as well as the medium for preservation of information. In India, we always need good instructional and enrichment films available in the international market. But there are hurdles in their import Even for the academic and research purposes. This requires urgent attention of all concerned so that motion picture can also be imported like books for the purpose of education and research. Moreover, just as there are renowned authors so are there well known filmmakers who have a series of worthwhile films to their credit and which could be an intrinsic part of every library.

Cinematographic film consists of a transparent flexible support or base on which is laid a photosensitive adhesive emulsion. They are now available in different widths ranging from 8 mm to 70 mm. The more the width the higher is the cost of the film. They are used for varied purposes depending upon the cost and the quality of the film. The super 8 mm is used very rarely as the infrastructure for production on this format is not generally available. But this is certainly the cheapest cinematographic medium available so far. The 16 mm film is used by most of the institutions for education and development. This has advantage over 8 mm because of comparatively higher resolution being suitable to be magnified on slightly larger screen.

Both the 8 mm and' 16 mm films are used depending upon the size of the audience as well as the cost of the production involved. The 35 mm and 70 mm films are normally used for entertainment and commercial purposes. 'They are suitable for larger gatherings like the audience of feature films in cinema halls. The advertisement agencies produce ads on these formats. The advantage of their having larger width is that the picture contain: very high resolution and does not blow up while magnified on larger screens. Sound for cinematographic films can be recorded magnetically or optically depending upon the circumstances.

Computer

Computer is regarded as the greatest invention of all the times. It facilitates the storage, processing and distribution of information much easier with its vast memory speed and accuracy. The advancements in calculator, which was invented to carry out mathematical calculations led to the invention of computer.

A more visible change took place when calculators acquired the capability of processing textual data proceeded by the capacity to process information available in varied formats. Further improvements in computer design during the 1960s enabled the integration of text and graphics, a move that encouraged the development of computer based training programs. Such use was however limited, as programming was costly, slow and cumbersome, and the computing relied on a mainframe, or central computer to do all the work. The release of the first microcomputers during the late 1970s saw computing become more portable and affordable. Ease of use took a quantum leap with the introduction of the Apple Macintosh computer in 1984. Operation of the computer and its programs became more intuitive, largely as a result of research in the area of human-computer interaction.

The adoption of computers in the area of vocational training also increased, with some industries recognising that the technology offered benefits that were largely cantered on efficiency gains. This was particularly the case in industries such as finance and insurance, manufacturing, health care, and the armed forces where training was a critical but costly component of operation. These types of organisations, with large staff numbers requiring training to an industry standard, or with staff located across national and international borders, found cost savings could be achieved by using technology to distribute training programs to the workplace, rather than bring staff to a central training centre. Computer programs could deliver training at a time and place convenient to all parties, provide flexibility in terms of progression and pace, generate and score tests, record all interaction between the learner and the system and produce detailed reports of this interaction. These attributes were welcomed in organisations where staff development programs were valued as a means of motivating staff and maintaining the standard of service. These programs are commonly based on competency standards that clearly define objectives, and set standards of performance that may be observed and measured against defined criteria.

The notion of providing training when it was needed to where it was needed was extended through the development of performance support systems. These systems allowed an employee to use a computer as both a tool and a tutor - the tutor would provide step by step assistance in the performance of specific computer related tasks, in much the same way as help "wizards" incorporated within many Microsoft products try to anticipate users needs in designing a new spreadsheet or database.

Computer based training has also been a logical choice where there was substantial risk in allowing a novice to train in an operational environment. It is safer and more cost effective to allow the operator of a steel rolling mill to practice the procedure using a computer simulation, or a pilot to manage an engine failure without leaving the ground. Submariners crewing the Australian Navy's new Collins Class submarines were expected to develop a familiarity of the control systems prior to the vessels delivery, again through the use of computer simulations. Adoption of computers in education has not always met with similar success. The reasons are varied, and these will be discussed in the next section. Computers can be an asset in education, but the knowledge of appropriate applications, limitations and advantage needs to be clearly understood.

Electronic Media

The electronic media has the capability to store, manipulate and transfer information in the form of text as well as audio visuals. It is also possible to combine both of them. Multimedia is and hypermedia can be cited as examples. The electronic media is useful in learning both in a classroom situation or individually. It includes information networks and CD ROMs. the information is recorded electronically, hence greater speed, accuracy and memory is available to the users. It is presumed that within the coming decade, the electronic media will supersede all the available media for storage, management and dissemination of information. This will particularly affect the educational institutions as it is more effective and economic both in terms of money and time spent in learning. It will also affect the nature of classroom instruction. A new learning culture is in the offing, which can be seen in the open system of education where attendance in class is not a prerequisite to earn a degree.

The advances in electronics and telecommunications brought newer technology capable of accommodating very large quantities of information in a very little space. Magnetic tapes, CD-ROMs, multimedia and hypermedia are a few examples. The capacity may be doubled if the stacks are partitioned according to the size of the disc and not the size of books which require more space. CD ROMs have the capacity to record and display large amount of information through computer system. The information contained in them can be manipulated and produced in varied sequences. They are easy to consult and make the searches convenient. The Microsoft Corporation has come out with a set of two CD ROMs that contains information equal to about twenty encyclopedia and the information it holds can be searched through various options.

CD ROMs have an edge on print as well as online resources. On the one hand they save a lot of physical space required for their print counterpart while on the other hand they allow to work on huge resources independent of online connectivity that is far expensive. The ever-increasing cost of Internet connectivity also suggests that CD ROM technology is more suited to education and research. Document in an ever-increasing number are being directly published on CD ROMs without involving prints. Now experts believe that the shift from page to screen once a fantasy is approaching reality now. Students in many university use textbook that exist online. Similarly there are CD ROMs, which hold valuable academic information and are the only sources of information in certain areas of study like medicine and technology.

In the electronic media, search time has been reduced miraculously. Bulky reference tools like the *Chemical Abstracts, Dissertation Index, Index to Higher Theses*, encyclopedias and dictionaries, etc. can be searched within a fraction of a second by just pushing the keys of a computer. Further, the search is very easy as most of the databases are user friendly. Any of the related words can be taken as 'Search Term' and fed into the system for retrieval of information. This is followed by appearance of a detailed list of documents available on the same topic from which one can select the most relevant and pinpointed information and even download it in the memory of the computer or on auxiliary memory for future use. There are some restrictions. Words, which can create hindrance are debarred from the retrieval process. They are called stop words. This is achieved by maintaining a separate file for them.

Another advantage of electronic media is the updating of the reference tools. Unlike the printed medium, which requires repeating the whole mechanical process for improvement or updating, the information is updated instantly in the electronic media. This is achieved with the push of a button. In fact, the agencies dealing in the electronic sources of information enter into an agreement with the consumers. The same discs can be sent to the agencies and returned updated. Now, with the Electronic Mail facility, updating can be carried out instantly on line. 'This practically involves no time and saves expenditure as well. In the print as well as the celluloid, mass copying leads to deterioration of prints by way of generation loss. But in the electronic media, the same text can be generated again and again without any loss or deterioration in the quality of the original or its copy.

In a tropical country like India the fluctuation in temperature and humidity leads to deterioration in the quality of print as well as celluloid by way of chemical reactions. This process of degeneration goes on with the passage of time. It is very difficult to maintain quality of print beyond a century and of celluloid beyond a decade. The solution lies to some extent in erection of specialized dehumidified chambers and providing air conditioners but this too is not practicable for many other reasons such as frequent breakdowns in supply of electricity and the huge expenditure involved.

Multimedia

Multimedia represents the convergence between computers, digital video, digital audio and sound synthesis. It has initially culminated the re-evaluation of the ways in which we communicate information combining still and moving images, sound, text and audio. Day to day applications of multimedia can be visualized considering information activities around us. Multimedia is being increasingly adopted for education and training, reference, business, entertainment etc.

Multimedia is widely acknowledged as an environment with great potentiality for education. It is able to assist both the people and teachers in new ways since for teacher it provides a means of putting across information and ideal and for students it can represent a one-to-one teaching environment which moves at the required pace.

Distribution of multimedia lessons, lectures and courseware on CD ROM or CD-1 discs adds another dimension to multimedia in education providing a vehicle of information to the students to take home. Its potential is enormous for the rural communities and isolated geographical regions where schools are inaccessible. The Open University teaching will certainly depend more upon the means and methods presented by advances in multimedia in the time to come.

As projected in the past we have now libraries without space. An information specialist sitting comfortably at his place of work just connecting his computer can establish contact with the desired number of foreign databases and an interaction can follow for the desired information. These services are being offered now on commercial basis too. The information thus selected can be downloaded on computer for further use.

Pupils traveled long distances in the past in search of information. Now information is knocking at their doors. The electronic devices have made it possible to transfer information at the speed of light. Pictures and sounds too are being transmitted from one place to the other. What is important today, is the selection of information and its dissemination for application. The quantum of information available is so much that everybody can have enough to learn individually. This is because of the coordination of efforts at the global level and presentation of this vast amount of information in a way that makes it convenient for the users to determine what is relevant to their needs.

Many academic institutions in the West have made database search an integral part of their educational process. Now thanks to the power of CD-ROM technology, information on nearly all the disciplines of education is available within reach of virtually every academic institution, its teachers, students and researchers. One can search as broadly, as deeply and as long as he or she wishes. The Indian National Scientific Documentation Centre is providing professional expertise in this regard to the academic and research institutions in India. Some other agencies like the Videsh Sanchar Nigam, the National Informatics Centre and the Faxon Informatics, Bangalore also coordinate in subscribing to these services. The data available from these agencies reveals steady growth in demand of the On-Line Information Services by the academic institutions in India.

The electronic media allows portability as well as durability. Information recorded digitally can last for centuries virtually with no effect of humidity, dust or temperature. The quality of recording is not affected because the information i , not recorded on the surface but within the medium itself. The electronic media seems to be ideal for preservation of manuscripts and other valuable records. There are two ways of recording from paper on to the digital media-one is the transfer of text page wise and the other is that the contents of rare manuscripts may be entered word by word. Thus, not only the life of the documents increases but also they can be retrieved rapidly and made available to the researchers.

The present situation has become an ideal one for adoption of Internet as in the words of Bill Gates "For the first time, all kinds of information-numbers, text sound video-can be put into a digital form that any computer can now store, process and forward. For the first time, standard hardware combined with a standard software platform has created economies of scale that make powerful computing solutions available extensively to all kinds of companies" (Business @ the speed of thought: Penguin Books: London (1999).

The confluence of satellite and multimedia resulted in making the communication technology available at an unimaginably lower cost to the betterment of the common man although it originated in labs for scientific researchers.

Now, Internet services are primarily based on these technologies.

As projected in the past we have now libraries without space. An information specialist sitting comfortably at his place of work just connecting his computer can establish contact with the desired number of foreign databases and an interaction can follow for the desired information. These services are being offered now on commercial basis too. The information thus selected can be downloaded on computer for further use.

Pupils traveled long distances in the past in search of information. Now information is knocking at their doors. The electronic devices have made it possible to transfer information at the speed of light. Pictures and sounds too are being transmitted from one place to the other. What is important today, is the selection of information and its dissemination for application. The quantum of information available is so much that everybody can have enough to learn individually. This is because of the coordination of efforts at the global level and presentation of this vast amount of information in a way that makes it convenient for the users to determine what is relevant to their needs.

Many academic institutions in the West have made database search an integral part of their educational process. Now thanks to the power of CD-ROM technology, information on nearly all the disciplines of education is available within reach of virtually every academic institution, its teachers, students and researchers. One can search as broadly, as deeply and as long as he or she wishes. The Indian National Scientific Documentation Centre is providing professional expertise in this regard to the academic and research institutions in India. Some other agencies like the Videsh Sanchar Nigam, the National Informatics Centre and the Faxon Informatics, Bangalore also coordinate in subscribing to these services. The data available from these agencies reveals steady growth in demand of the On-Line Information Services by the academic institutions in India.

The electronic media allows portability as well as durability. Information recorded digitally can last for centuries virtually with no effect of humidity, dust or temperature. The quality of recording is not affected because the information i , not recorded on the surface but within the medium itself. The electronic media seems to be ideal for preservation of manuscripts and other valuable records. There are two ways of recording from paper on to the digital media-one is the transfer of text page wise and the other is that the contents of rare manuscripts may be entered word by word. Thus, not only the life of the documents increases but also they can be retrieved rapidly and made available to the researchers.

The present situation has become an ideal one for adoption of Internet as in the words of Bill Gates "For the first time, all kinds of information-numbers, text sound video-can be put into a digital form that any computer can now store, process and forward. For the first time, standard hardware combined with a standard software platform has created economies of scale that make powerful computing solutions available extensively to all kinds of companies" (Business @ the speed of thought: Penguin Books: London (1999).

The Internet

Internet has emerged as the most powerful medium for storage and retrieval of information. It works round the clock and connects every nook and corner of the globe. With an unprecedented growth in the quantum of knowledge worldwide and the easy accessibility, Internet has become an unavoidable necessity for every institution of higher learning and research. Internet is continuously growing internationally. Within a short span of ten years, its services have been spread among all the nations of the world. In 1991 it was within reach of 73 countries but within four years of its existence Internet reached 148 countries. The number of Internet users is also increasing tremendously as they are almost doubled after every two years. In the meanwhile Internet widened its scope. Now it is used for storage, manipulation and dissemination of textual data as well as the multimedia.

Internet became more popular by its feature of the World Wide Web in 1991, Tim Berners-Lee, a young scientist working in European Particle Physics Laboratory (CERN) produced Internet's first browser. According to him, "the dream behind the Web is of a common information space in which we communicate by sharing information. "By its application, someone could scan every document or photo or video on the net. It gave an opportunity to share the resources by individuals and organizations on the basis of mutual understanding. In the past ten years, it has been so popular that the number of Internet users has jumped from 600,000 to 140 million and it is expected to grow further to 350 millions within the next three years.

With the increasing dependant on micro literature for research in the universities and the availability of improved technology for information handling, the traditional library practices of classification and cataloguing are proving to be less relevant. As the information needs of users even in the academic institutions are satisfied with some alternate means. The growing use of Internet by medical and engineering institutions is a clear indication of what is in store for the libraries of the future? PUBMED, a service of the National Library of Medicine provides access to over 11 millions of citations back to the mid 1960s and additional life science journals. It includes links to many similar websites providing fall text articles and other related resources. The service is available free of cost. Journals are the most pertinent sources of information for research in the universities. They are available in plenty on Internet. Moreover a large number of them is free of cost and if priced they cost less compared to their print counterpart. After the print media, journals could not figure in any other format except the digital media. The audiovisuals remained short lived and barring a few political ones no worth mentioning journal could surface in the audiovisual media.

Internet has also democratized the process of higher education in the true sense librating it from the clutches of the few knowledgeable and powerful without whom research was a distant dream for the students. It has affected almost every sphere of human activities. In the field of education, the work of traditional gurus has been taken over by Internet now, which provides information on the latest advancements and researches taking place in the various disciplines of study. It also supports farther activities of collecting data, analyzing and synthesizing it. Moreover it presents the events in international perspective hence the research work is supposed to be unique whereas the chances for repetition were higher in the past when things were perceived in the limited geographical limits.

Virtual Universities

With increasing convergence between computer and communication technologies and the spread of communication networks the present day open universities are expected to gradually transform themselves as virtual universities, where almost all functions of the university take place electronically over digital links and networks.

In Indian universities have started a beginning for which the following possibilities may be forecasted for the time to come:

* Pre-eminence of the printed text as the master medium of instruction will gradually yield place to multi-media instruction through CD-ROMs and such other devices.
* Audio and video programmes which are now tape-based will enjoy disc based digital storage techniques for deterioration free preservation and random on-demand retrieval through network
* Broad-band digital communication through satellite

will be used for synchronous and asynchronous interactivity between teachers and students and among students groups located in different places.

* Internet will play an increasingly central role in the university functioning right from student admission, programme delivery, counseling and assignments to final evaluation and certificates.
* The present day study centers would transform themselves to function more as kiosks offering information and communication terminals to students rather than as places where face to face counseling is conducted. A medium of face to face component may still continue, but more for social interaction than academic purposes.

3
University Libraries of the Future

The 21st century has just started and it has to go a long way with a fast changing information scenario. There is a fear among librarians as how to plan for and cope with the future. This fear and hope for the future is a natural human response to the unknown since we inherit traditional systems almost in every sphere of our activities which are deeply rooted to resist any change. In a virtual golden age of science and technology where we live for almost a century, people still believe in superstitions and seek their fortunes in a great number. Humans are itching to know the unknowable, and nothing is more unknowable than what will happen tomorrow.

It seems particularly appropriate to examine this urge at the dawn of a new millennium. The 20th century may be looked as a touchstone for those seeking to predict the future. A study of predictions over the last several hundred years reveals some distinct changes in how humans have viewed the future, from shining utopia to space-age paradise to darker forecasts. The rapid changes in technology and society that defined the Industrial Revolution of the 19th century created a ripe environment for futuristic projection almost in every sphere of activities.

Education has been a major concern for predictions with the fast changing scenario all over the world. At the higher level, it is has been described more as a process of learning than of teaching. It is primarily based on self-efforts by students under the guidance of teachers. Therefore, students are provided with necessary facilities for mastering the subject matter, techniques, skills, habits of thought and methods of working the selected field of study. Such requirements cannot be fulfilled with classroom teaching since a lot of work depends upon the support of research materials, which are housed in libraries.

While discussing the future of libraries we should go deep into their past and take a glance at the libraries so that the future may be predicted in a better way. In the 13th century, monks reproduced information by hand in a room called the scriptorium. Each book, a process of many years of labour, then went into the monastic libraries where they were chained to the shelves to guard against theft or unauthorized copying. In the 15th century, with the invention of the printing press, books lost their chains, and monasteries lost their monopoly on information. But it took several hundred years before libraries became what many take for granted today: public institutions, which guarantee any citizen access to information without charge. In the 19th century, the United States led the way, guaranteeing its citizens access to information through public libraries. But in current century seems to replace all such restrictions on the seekers of knowledge and also relieving them of the pains they experienced in the past in getting the required information.

Now, knowledge is expanding at a tremendous speed as a result of increased research activities affecting almost every field of human activities. University stands for teaching, research, extension and publication of ideas. Library is an essential organ of an educational institution specially the institution of higher learning. It plays prominent role in supporting the higher education and fulfilling its objectives. The status of a library can well be judged by the remarks of the Kothari Commission which states "no university or college or department should be set up without taking into account its library needs in terms of staff, books, journals etc. Nothing could be more damaging to a growing department than to neglect its library or give it a low priority. On the contrary, the library should be an important centre of attraction on the college or university campus".

A glance at the development in the last century shows that the university libraries in India not only grew exponentially but also their services were recognized at the international level. Dr. S. R. Ranganathan made a great contribution to the field and proved that the Indian techniques of dealing with the knowledge and information were not inferior to any other country in the world.

The present university Library system was designed by previous generation of librarians in response to the prevailing conditions at that time. The system responded to the situation well but it needs changes in the present perspective and also to cope with the future needs when a number of IT gadgets are available to provide still better services at a lower cost. The impact of technology is clearly visible on university libraries since they are very closely linked with the developmental activities.

Libraries have undergone drastic changes in respect of their architecture, nature of holdings and also the services. All of them contribute to the change in the way of their functioning. It is not possible now for a single library to acquire or accommodate all the information resources being generated internationally, regionally or even in a given subject and they are making provisions for sharing of resources in increasing proportions.

Now, libraries are well connected within their fore walls as well as with the outside world. They have responded to the crisis of increasing demands and limited resources through a greater reliance on rationalization, cooperation and networking. The major initiatives in this area include the Regional Public Library Systems and the automated resource sharing networks, both of which provide libraries with expanded access to materials and information not available locally.

As we enter the 21st century, libraries must continue to serve as intellectual and cultural centers for their communities by maintaining strong collections of books and periodicals. At the same time, they must also provide access to an expanding world of information and keep pace with changes in information technology. It is clear that libraries can and will play a critical role to meet the challenges of the future, but their ability to do so effectively will be determined by the a number of issues.

Impact of Technology

The dawn of the 21st century has brought with it tremendous potential for further raising our standard of living because of the advancement in production and exchange of information. At the end of the 20th century, Alvin Toffler termed information technology as the 'ultimate technology' and his phrase comes true even today whereas there has been a great upheaval in the world of information during the last fifty years and many technologies such as the technology of audiovisuals died an untimely death. The rapid emergence of multimedia and CD ROM materials has its way defined the change from analog to digital systems, and along with the change has come increasingly pervasive emphasis on computer based technologies and multimedia design and access.

The application of information technologies enlarges the scope of knowledge acquisition, rises speed and reduces cost. It is impossible to accomplish such important tasks by using man's brains only in the modern society in which the knowledge changes with each passing day. It will be possible to link closely knowledge sources and knowledge workers by computer networks, thus constructing knowledge networks in.

Computer is, perhaps the most significant invention of man after the wheel. It revolutionized the process of collection, storage and dissemination of information and when coupled with the power of telecommunication it affected almost every sphere of human society. It not only allowed the transformation of society at a higher pace but also contributed to the scientific and technological development.

The impact of information technology on the academic libraries, especially the university libraries have been unparallel. Now, in view of the tremendous potential of technology, a number of organizations support the advancement of university libraries at the national as well as the international level like UNESCO, ERNET, INSDOC, DESIDOC, AICTE, Department of Electronics and Planning Commission. The University Grants Commission besides offering funds also helps the university libraries in the modernization process in other ways also.

The Information and Library Network (INFLIBNET) Project was launched in the decade of eighties with the objective of resource sharing for reduction of expenditure and providing better library services for all the universities and other major institutions of higher learning. Now, a number of other information networks including ERNET, DELNET, CALIBNET, INFONET etc have emerged at the scene, which contribute towards better library services in a networked environment.

The task of computerization has become simpler comparing with the last century when such user friendly software were not available although the hardware was suitably developed to cope with the needs of the university libraries. In the changed circumstances of today, the energy of the library should not be wasted merely in creating the databases of their respective holding alone but more emphasis should be given now on sharing information with other organizations and making the optimum use of the information resources available freely on the World Wide Web. In certain areas like health and education, a lot of literature is available freely on the Internet, which might be used by the university libraries besides the utilization of paid services.

Future Technologies

The main information technologies relevant to libraries in the time to come will include: Internet, Intranet and Extranet; storage architectures; database management systems; metadata; data acquisition and gathering; dissemination, messaging; push and pull; information retrieval; information resources sharing; groupware; middleware; on-line analytical processing; multidimensional analysis and data mining. Nanotechnology is also emerging fast with a vast potential of changing the information scenario. These technologies should be adopted for better results in the university libraries.

Internet has already revolutionized the world of information. It is one of the two technological innovations that have greatly influenced the development of communication strategies and practices in both the general and the business communities of the world. The first innovation was the invention of the printing press by Johan Gutenberg around 1450 in Mainz, Germany. Gutenberg's invention served to democratize the possession and transmission of texts, for it made the production of books much easier and, thereby, much cheaper than did the manuscript method it replaced. A little over four hundred years after Gutenberg began printing books with his press, Alexander Graham Bell invented the first telephone for practical use.

Another significant change in the libraries is being brought by the inception of digital libraries. Digital libraries are the current innovations which came into being as a result of technological advancements in the field of electronics engineering as well as the changing requirements and expectations from the traditional libraries. They are also referred as the collections of information stored in digital format and accessible over a communication network. Digital libraries are developing fast at the national and international levels. A number of projects have been undertaken at the national as well as international level in the specific areas of knowledge. The Universal Digital Library and the Digital Library of India projects are worth mentioning here. The former is a cooperative Indo-US Project, which aims at digitizing one million books at the first instance. Indian scientists have been an active force behind this project.

Changing Nature of Information

Reduction in the number of print acquisitions has resulted in increasing reliance on the other documents containing information. Celluloid was once an effective medium for information, specially education and entertainment. The advent of video accelerated its use whereas the multimedia has overtaken it in about all the activities relating to the fulfillment of the information needs of the society.

Apart from a large number of books and journals, most of the reference books are being published on the web for some years. Several hundred dictionaries are freely available. Many specialist encyclopedias and subject reference works have been converted to become experimental web services. Although there are many good reference books on the web, the experimental and haphazard fashion in which they have been launched means that they are not as useful or as 'findable' as one might wish. The lack of system is particularly wasteful in the case of reference resources. Their evaluation in the library should form a major activity..

The commercial publishers see the potential of web delivery. Several of them have converted their most important reference works into web-based reference services, backed by professional promotion and customer support. There have already been some notable achievements: The Oxford English Dictionary, the Grove Dictionary of Art, and the large reference works published by the Gale Group are pioneers in this gradual mobilization of reference resources to the worldwide web. So far all the clear-cut commercial successes have been large books, which in their web implementation are offered to subscribers (mainly institutions with libraries) for an annual subscription.

The information is being published on the World Wide Web in greater quantity nowadays than in the print media for varied purposes and almost in all the disciplines of study. There are precedents for aggregating published reference works: Infoplease and Bartleby are both examples of popular consumer-oriented web services.

Cooperation among University Libraries

No single library can accumulate the information resources being generated internationally and even within a particular country. Now, individual libraries increasingly rely on cooperation and networking. It has become clear that libraries of all types need to work together much more closely if they are to meet all the information needs of users. Libraries are used more conveniently by varied type of users. If libraries are to meet the rapidly changing needs of residents in the future, they must have cooperative structures, which allow them to connect users with the widest range of possible resources, regardless of which type of library provides this connection.

Various international agencies including UNESCO and the Commonwealth have supported cooperation between libraries including some support for shared automated networks at international level. Some other agencies are also trying to achieve coordination at the national level. But what is needed beyond these successful programs is an overall structure to promote cooperation and improved access to information among all libraries on international level. State-supported programs for cooperation and networking among different types of libraries are currently in place in almost every other state, and are particularly well developed in states with technology-oriented economies. A statewide structure for cooperation would make more of these specialized resources accessible through libraries to businesses and individuals who do not currently have ready access to them.

Statewide access to computerized information requires an "information highway" which will link libraries and library users with online electronic information sources. Initiatives at the national level (the National Research and Education Network, or NREN) and the New England regional level provide the backbone telecommunications system (known collectively as the Internet) necessary for the provision of electronic information resources to libraries. However, a network linking all libraries to these regional and national networks is essential in order to provide the full range of electronic information resources.

In the face of the bleak university funding outlook, university libraries world over are leading the way to a cooperative information future. It will enhance students' and researchers' access to knowledge. Such an alliance will improve the academic information infrastructure and ensure that university libraries being vital organizations are able to underpin research and teaching activities in the increasingly competitive higher education environment.

Universities are driving an agenda for a strong, cooperative, networked university library system supported by a powerful range of programs expanding information access and exchange. These programs include: intelligent Internet gateways to information for major subject disciplines; a series of national benchmarks; a cooperative, national digital and print archive and store; negotiation of improved licensing conditions for access to electronic journals and databases; a national reciprocal borrowing scheme; strategic partnerships to enhance access to knowledge; and increased cooperative purchasing. The broad aims are to make the most of limited resources by: maximising purchasing power; expanding resource sharing; and finding new models for preservation, storage and access to university research resources.

Steps undertaken in this direction include the development of electronic gateways to information in various specialized areas of knowledge specially agriculture, medicine and technology whereby any researcher or student needs only one password for access to all eligible electronic resources.

Collection Development

Collection development activities in libraries cover a wide area of activities. It is one of the most significant practices upon which depends the utility of the library resources. A carefully built small collection of a library can be more effective than the casually developed larger collections. The traditional collections of libraries are primarily based on the print media but in the time to come more and more emphasis will be given to the electronic media and specially the resources being offered through Internet.

All disciplines are experiencing changes in scholarly communication in a variety of ways and at significantly different rates. Each discipline still relies on published journals for current awareness, but some disciplines have better access to electronic versions of both current and retrospective research materials than others. A few disciplines are creating resources that are not surrogates of paper products.

Books and journals are the most common sources of information available in the university libraries. They are selected for purchase in the library through various methods and employing various means. The most common approach is the selection of general books by librarians and the subject related literature by the heads of the various departments of study. A number of selection tools are available for this purpose including trade bibliographies, catalogues of publishers, list of suppliers, reviews as appeared in periodical publications etc. A lot of literature is available in the Net nowadays. The most significant website apart from the various bibliographies, catalogues and union lists for selection of documents is a website. www.amazon.com. It may be searched to obtain details of books and other educational media in various academic disciplines. OPAC is a computerized library catalog available to the public. OPAC are designed for an individual library and consulted within its building or it may be made available outside the library through Intranet and Internet also. These days most OPACs are accessible over the Internet to users all over the world.

At the dawn of the 21st century, many of the academic libraries have been offering facility for online access. The trend will grow positively with the new media being available easily and economically day by day offering more and more information resources in varying formats. The university libraries should form a part of the fibre optic-based campus-LAN having Information Outlets (IOs) which links a computing node to the Campus LAN and to the Internet. They should also have their own sub-LAN consisting of terminals, terminal controllers and servers to support OPAC services and other in-house computerization activities within the Library. The terminals in the Library can also be used for Internet access in textual mode using Lynx browser:

The scholarly research requires timely and efficient access to information resources. Libraries have previously functioned as repositories for collections, the collection is already moving well beyond the boundaries of library walls. The digitization of statistical data sources and the production of electronic journals are precursors to new and rapidly developing forms of scholarly communication. Initiatives at scores of other academic institutions point the way to increased reliance on computers and networks for storage, access and manipulation of both primary and secondary sources of research.

The IP enabled access to JSTOR Arts and Sciences Collection I & II has been set up by some university libraries for students and other users as in case of the Jawahalal Nehru University in New Delhi for the Campus Network. This service is regulated through a grant from Ford Foundation. Thus the university libraries have an access to a number e-portals for journals spanning many disciplines such as Science Online, J-Gate, Annual Reviews, Kluwer e-journals etc.

Resource Generation

University libraries can no longer be viewed as passive and non-profit organizations since they accommodate resources purchased out of a huge amount of money and brought out over a long period by the best brain in subject fields. Unfortunately, most of the university libraries are not generating their own revenues. On the one hand the expenses on university libraries can be minimized with the adoption of new technology whereas on the other hand, revenues may be generated within the libraries.

The process of privatization of education has been accelerated in India as in the other advanced countries. The university libraries should grab the opportunity not only for their survival but also making their services more effective. Dr. Thompson in his book 'Library Power" refers to this point *"Libraries are institutions charged with the duty of providing the means for the perpetual self education of one and all, and then contribute to the circulation of ideas, the demand of democracy, the spread of literacy and the success of commercial and industrial enterprises".*

The university libraries have a tremendous potential to provide services to the business and industrial houses of their areas and to earn money from them. This earning can be used in strengthening of the library services at a comparatively low cost for the academic community. This can be achieved by properly informing the relevant user groups of the materials available on their demands and such demands can be recorded in the form of their user profiles.

On the pattern of some other institutions especially the Indian Institutes of Technology, the university libraries should launch individual membership for private consultant and professionals who are not affiliated to any corporate organization and thus are not eligible for corporate membership. The individual membership would only be offered to qualified professionals in engineering and technology and academicians from other fields after their applications are scrutinizing by the Senior Library Officers Committee. The Individual Membership may available against annual payment. The Individual Members can be allowed consultation facilities. They can also be allowed to use other library services.

User Education

Effectively using electronic sources produced commercially or informally on the Internet has become a challenge for scholars. Libraries provide guidance and instruction in the productive and effective use of these materials. For example, library staff provide web-based guides, group instruction, or individual instruction.

In the time to come the role of librarian will change. Training of users will become a major activity in the university libraries for them since every body will have enough amount of information within reach and only the retrieving techniques will be needed to obtain it.

User education is imparted in libraries to support the seekers of information to explain the techniques of information storage and retrieval so that they could be made self-dependent or less dependent in matters of locating the information. The practice continued in the past and still there are some institutions, which impart user education. Perhaps there is no university library barring a few agriculture universities where such education is being imparted in an organized way.

It is strange to note that at the time when information was confined mainly to books and journals and the process of information was also easier compared with the present day situation, user education was being imparted by some university libraries. Now, with the ever increasing complications resulting from the arrival of a vide array of information products and more dependence on scientific instruments for retrieval of information that have come in the way of users, no due weight is being given to it.

University libraries should design courses on user education and impart training to the students and faculty. Library is the most appropriate place for such an activity since it is better equipped with the information retrieval machinery in comparison of any other department of study. Even the departments of library and information studies do not possess such facilities to demonstrate the practical procedure of information retrieval.

Library Staff

It firstly requires that leaders who take charge of the university library should undertake to formulate the management plans and coordinate all knowledge management related activities. Secondly, it requires establishment of special leading groups of knowledge flow for accomplishing all tasks relating to the university libraries. Electronic resources committees should be established composed of various types of specialists to take charge of evaluating, procuring and creating the electronic resources on the one hand, and coordinating activities of business departments and spurring them on to close cooperation in such fields as procurement and organization of the electronic information resources as well as providing services on the other hand.

Human resources management takes it as its basic starting point to train high quality specialized talents and to revitalize the library undertaking. In practice, we should pay full attention to diversity and variation of library staffs' requirements, strengthened management of different library staffs by applying contingency management approach. That is, to some people, rigid management method is applied, rigorous supervision and control imposed, and quantity and quality requirements of work according to regulations and procedures are made clear. And, to the rest of people, more flexible management method is applied to let them participate in decision-making and consultation and undertake more jobs so as to bring their management abilities into full play and realize organizational and personal objectives. Doing well in continuous education of specialized staffs, which should not only focus on the theory of library science and related disciplines, but also cover the latest technical knowledge.

End users of the new electronic information systems will require considerable assistance and training. The users will also need knowledgeable librarians to assist them in locating information and learning new skills. A seamless transition between searching for and receiving the necessary information is not yet a reality. Information specialists are required to assess and select the best search tools (regardless of format) and to integrate these tools with local service. Instructing users to search using a wide range of tools is a formidable task during a time of transition. From developing computerized course packs in support of distance education to providing web guides for researchers, Information Resources staff will continue to devise and facilitate new forms of instruction to meet these challenges.

Professional development is the ongoing responsibility of all librarians to maintain current skills, develop new skills, and to implement the information services needed in a constantly changing environment. To support this development the libraries generally provide in-service training for librarians, encourage and support attendance at other professional programs, and provide the appropriate equipment suitable for service at the highest level. The Libraries will continue to provide, on a systemwide basis, workshops and other formal programs designed to help librarians keep abreast of new technologies and other advances and to maintain traditional skills at a high level. Such programs should include both in-house and external experts.

University libraries possess the creamy layer of the library professionals since they are recruited on the guidelines approved for the teachers. Still the eligibility condition for an Assistant Librarian's post is NET/Ph. D. in library and information science. Library professionals from other fields always looked for jobs in the university libraries in view of the better prospects. This practice is still continuing but such promotional avenues and other facilities provided to the librarians have been denied by the Fifth Pay Commission depriving them of their earlier status at par with the teaching staff.

Future Projections

The projected results of future developments in case of the university libraries suggest that the new media will take over the existing dominance of the print media within the coming 50 years. The trend is visible even today in few disciplines of knowledge where greater emphasis is given to the World Wide Web offer collection of information on certain topics. In fact, the field of medicine, education and other social science discipline are well covered by the new media a lot of which is readily available free of cost.

With most of the new innovations and increasingly new publications being directly produced in the new electronic media, efforts are being made at all levels to transform existing textbooks into digital media. Once it is accomplished the potential from them is likely to be greater because such a change will promote their use globally and by a greater number of users simultaneously. Likewise the other media of communication in its individual form will also have wider implications for the academic world.

Digital libraries are emerging as the future avtaars of the present day libraries. Most of them are in the process of making and are generally being developed in isolation by a number of organizations specially the educational institutions all over the world like the inception of the Universal Digital Library, an Indo-US venture. Once developed and connected, the digital libraries will supercede all the traditional libraries of today reducing them to merely the museum of books and it is going to be happened within a short span of time since their vast capacity of accommodating resources, speed of information retrieval and accuracy in operations they offer is unparallel to the existing type of libraries.

University libraries of the future will not require large buildings as they have today. With further expansion of Internet facilities, the largest libraries of the world are available at one's desk. Information on any subject can be drawn on the desktop of computers within a short time from any corner of the world at a cheaper cost and the limitations of time and space come nowhere in the process.

The role of librarians will also change from merely selection of books and journals and maintaining the traditional services but also they will become active partner in the modernization process; planning and implementing ideas in the changed requirements of the day. Now seemingly for the first time librarians are selecting data, still and moving images and audiovisual images from various sources near and far. They are also customizing the information resources for the users such as by developing the multimedia kits. Their active participation is necessary in all these activities for survival also else the profession will be overtaken by the specialist from the related field. The new situation has drastically called for the training of librarians in the organization and management of the new information products and services and it is easier for them in comparison to any other profession since they are already in the relevant business.

There are some practices in the libraries, which are losing their significance like the classification and cataloguing. The various schemes of classification were promulgated to facilitate the retrieval of documents in view of the limitation of human memory in order to keep pace with the huge collection of books and also for coordination of concept so that the related subjects may be grouped together. But it is now being substituted by the vast amount of memory, speed and accuracy of the computer systems that can retrieve the required segments of information from a huge library collection and online databases. Similarly, in cataloguing, the entry element was vital to facilitate access but the required information can be accessed in any desired sequence. There are many points of access for retrieval on information from the new information media then they were available through the catalogue cards. In most of the modern university libraries, catalogue cards have already been replaced or sidelined by Online Public Access Catalogue (OPAC).

It is expected from the recent developments that the university libraries of the future will be entirely different in respect of their architecture, services and clientele. They will mainly rest in electronic form, will be used round the clock and cover the entire disciplines of study.

4
Education and the Digital Libraries

Changes are going on in the educational system all around the world. These changes are needed because of ever growing pressure in systems of education themselves, partly because society itself is changing into one in which knowledge work becomes ever more important, and partly because of the very information and communication technologies which are transforming our economies. Both of these factors evoke change and offer a solution to the problems with which the educational system struggles. Various surveys on education have revealed that one model developed in a country for education is application in the other country now which was never so in the past. It shows that a "global learning infrastructure" is emerging fast supported by the latest communication technologies in which the role of schools and universities will be drastically changed, a radical transformation of the educational system. The following trends are visible all over the world:

* The number of students is still growing.
* Different types of students are asking for education; participation of women, older students, and students from ethnic minorities is growing. Different students bring different experiences with them.
* Increasingly, work and study are combined, and that leads to a need for more flexible learning arrangements in which the campus or school building is no longer central to the educational process.

* More generally, there is a trend towards lifelong learning.
* Lifelong learning leads to an emphasis on "learning to learn". Knowledge becomes obsolete at an ever-increasing rate in a knowledge economy, and knowledge workers need to be able to refresh their knowledge on a regular basis.
* Because of the differences between students, there is a need to accommodate different learning styles, customization and alternative learning routes. Courses have to take more into account the different experiences and backgrounds of students.
* Higher education institutions have long had a monopoly in providing education, but increasingly, companies and public bodies possess knowledge that can be reused for educational purposes, partly for in-house training (knowledge management) but also to offer to external markets.
* Education is under constant budget pressure, thus there is a need for more efficient and effective education.
* Students more and more are behaving like consumers who want to make informed choices about how and where they want to be educated, which implies students are no longer committed to one institution.
* Teaching staff will exhibit more job-hopping behavior than they did in the past.
* There are too many dropouts in the current educational system.

Information and communication technologies (ICT) have the potential to offer a solution for at least part of the problems.

* Through the Internet, course material can be offered independently of time and place. Modularization makes it possible to offer different and flexible learning routes.
* An ever-increasing number of students have access to

the Internet, whether at home or on campus. Costs of Internet access will continue to drop.

* More and more information is made available through the web. Search engines assure the accessibility of this material. Groupware allows (a)synchronous communication between teachers and students — worldwide.
* Online market research is quick and easy, and this market information can be combined with transaction log data allowing institutions to monitor consumer (i.e., student) response on an ongoing basis.
* In principle, a worldwide competition for education is possible and it is already apparent in the market for MBA courses. There is an increasing competition in the delivery of information services for higher education, implying that libraries might lose their monopoly position in information services to their parent institutions. (Hughes' e-book company, Questia Media, is an example of a new competitor.)

In summary, one might envisage learning environments of the future as:

* being student-centered
* being interactive and dynamic
* enabling group work on real world problems
* enabling students to determine their own learning routes
* emphasizing competencies like information literacy to support lifelong learning

Through these elements listed above runs a common theme: the adoption of more active learning styles in which students take more responsibility for their own learning goals and for the ways in which to realize these objectives. Active learning implies that students don't limit themselves to resources supplied by their instructors, but also that the students search for new materials themselves in order to solve problems at hand and to develop their competencies continuously.

The Role of Digital Libraries

Since libraries are still actively supporting research and education, a relevant question is how libraries can and should transform themselves in order to cope with the changes in our educational systems. The following the five strategic areas to be discussed in this next:

* digital libraries and digital learning environments
* digital portfolios
* information literacy
* collaborative course design
* the relation between physical and virtual learning environments.

Digital libraries and digital learning environments

Digital libraries are able to integrate the freely available information on the web with the more formal literature for which licenses on electronic versions are arranged with publishers. These licenses enhance and replace traditional collection development policies. Digital libraries facilitate time and place independent information services for students, needed especially if active learning styles become more commonplace. Digital libraries are already available 24 hours a day and seven days a week from anywhere in the world, offering flexible arrangements for students/knowledge workers. Much work done over the past decade in developing digital libraries will have an important pay-off for educational innovation. The main issue, of course, is whether more active learning styles will become the norm, since many of today's courses are of a rather "self contained" nature in which educators present students with texts to work through in a linear way and assessment is too often based on whether or not a student is able to reproduce the texts prescribed by the teacher.

Two approaches in this respect can be identified. The first one, which takes the needs of specific courses as point of departure, can be seen mainly in the UK in projects like INSPIRAL and ResIDE. INSPIRAL is a research project in England that investigates issues involved in linking virtual or digital or managed learning environments with digital libraries. It looks at technical, institutional and end-user challenges, with an emphasis on the last two aspects, and analyzes stakeholders' and learners' needs. Its point of departure seems to be how teaching staff can best be supported when designing digital learning environments and enriching these environments with resources available in digital libraries. This tailor-made approach is very much apparent in the ResIDE project where the focus is on the teachers and their courses.

A more popular in the United States, has a different, more macro way of looking at digital library support for learning environments and concentrates on learning resources in general. An example of this approach is the National Science Foundation (NSF) national science, mathematics, engineering, and technology education digital library (NSDL) program. This program seeks to bring together a vast, centralized collection of learning resources supporting all possible kinds of education, ranging from K-12 to graduate and lifelong learning, into one big library for the nation and even beyond. As such, the NSDL approach is consistent with the large scale of many of the other NSF digital libraries projects.

The NSDL approach seems more threatening to libraries and librarians but in both options there will still be a need for library staff to support educators with respect to the selection of adequate resources for a given course.

Librarians pursuing this aspect are well advised to learn more about the standards (e.g., IMS / Instructional Management Systems) being developed to protect investments in content development from the rapid developments in technology used in digital learning environments. The issue here is that instructional content should be easily transferable from one platform to another. The main problem seems to be managerial short-sightedness. In the Netherlands, for example, the common opinion of administrators seems to be that work on digital libraries doesn't need special attention anymore for which some valid arguments can be put forward and that the subject of ICT in education is an entirely different one from the subject of digital libraries. The point, of course, is that this view fails to incorporate the advantages of digital libraries, which are natural complements to digital learning environments.

Student's Assessment

Digital portfolios are new tools for student assessment and they are more than that as well. Initially, digital portfolios were developed as an alternative way of assessing student progress, with more emphasis on the learning process and the material results a student achieves throughout a course of study. By showing material results, the student can demonstrate that certain competencies have been acquired. At the same time, as a personal tool the portfolio offers students the ability to closely monitor their own progress and to set new learning goals in the planning of their education. Additionally, a portfolio, which continues to grow during training, can be used in job interviews to show prospective employers the candidate's background in a much richer way. Digital portfolios work especially well in situations where students work with assignments to solve real-life problems and are free to manage their own learning process.

The digital portfolios are an extension of the first domain identified digital libraries and digital learning environments — but now include the intranet. The emphasis here is on the institution as a knowledge organization, and the integration of that knowledge with other information resources.

Information literacy

Adding digital portfolios to the ever increasing amount of information available leads to a third domain in which libraries can play a more active role in support of educational innovation: information literacy. The concept of information literacy can be traced back to the 1970s and was originally connected to democratic ideals. Throughout the years, the view of information literacy has evolved towards a more technical one and has been connected to the development of the information society, a term which is now being replaced by the notion of the knowledge economy. A well-known definition of information literacy is the one developed by the American Library Association as "Information literate are not only able to recognize when information is needed, but they are also able to identify, locate, evaluate, and use effectively information needed for the particular decision or issue at hand. The information literate person, therefore, is empowered for effective decision making, freedom of choice, and full participation in a democratic society."

Librarians are uniquely qualified to assume an active role in the new teaching environment because of their skills in collecting, evaluating, organizing and providing access to information. Information literacy can be seen as building on, but going way beyond, traditional library instruction. Increasingly, librarians will be involved in teaching classes — sometimes in close cooperation with faculty, sometimes in general skills courses. An important trend in the last few years is that library staffs are developing internet-based instruction modules. The Texas Information Literacy Tutorial <http://tilt.lib.utsystem.edu/> is an excellent example of this latter approach, which has gained widespread recognition in the library community.

Collaborative course design

Of course, librarians who are building expertise in developing web-based course material can also use this expertise in a more broad sense. The idea here is that in contrast with the traditional situation in which teaching staff develops courses on their own, and choose the way they teach and assess student progress (the teacher as king of his class) — learning environments of the future will be designed by multi-disciplinary teams of experts. Experts in developing course material, programmers, graphical designers, and experts in assessment, all will work together in designing rich modularized learning environments that offer alternative learning routes to different types of students. However, many learning environments build on a model for which origins can be traced back to early distance education. In this model, students are given a "box" containing all the material for a course they need to master, so-called self-contained courses. An approach that, of course, made sense in traditional distance education where library support has always been a rather cumbersome issue.

The digital learning environments lead some educators to use the technology to gain even more control over students. But if the emphasis is on developing competencies needed to become knowledge workers, and if work and learning are more interconnected, one might expect that learning environments will become more open. Students in such a model are expected to go beyond the primary learning materials offered by teaching staff and are expected to explore independently other information sources as well.

Again, if more active learning styles become the norm, then one can foresee a role for librarians in the multi-disciplinary teams developing learning environments such as those mentioned above. Librarians can add links to the resources — print and electronic — available in their collections and on the web. They can explain how information resources in a particular subject field are organized and how students can find their way in subject areas that are relatively new to them.

Physical and virtual learning environments

The virtual learning environments will suffice to satisfy the needs of future students. Students encounter many technical problems and miss the direct feedback inherent to class room situations where even the body language of the teacher gives important clues. Next to virtual learning environments, the physical learning environment will remain of importance too, and the two will probably coexist for generations to come. If we look at recent developments in library architecture in the United States, some trends in library functions become more visible. There is a clear trend towards more client-centered buildings instead of the collection-centered ones of the past. Some libraries experiment with lounge-like facilities and offer pleasant reading rooms, not just for individuals but also for groups.

Integration of libraries with computing facilities is a clear trend, one that will present even more of a challenge now that multimedia computers are becoming the norm. Increasingly, the term "learning environment" or "learning center" is used for this kind of facility. It shows that, next to digital learning environments, there is also a need for physical learning environments where students and teachers find a wealth of resources and facilities, and where they can work, on their own or together, in order to learn and teach.

Implications for library staff and organization

The linking of digital libraries to digital learning environments, standards issues, knowledge-sharing, support in education, more active support of educational processes, classroom instruction, development of course modules in multi disciplinary teams, rethinking and redesigning library buildings all these issues have obviously profound implications for library personnel. This requires a proactive approach: look at what is going on in education in your institution and show where library resources can enhance learning environments

On a larger scale, there could be organizational consequences. Much in the same way that digital library projects have led to closer cooperation, and sometimes mergers, between libraries and computer centers, educational innovation leads to closer cooperation between libraries, computer centers and educational support units. Another option is to explore the possibilities of networked organizations in order to mobilize and combine the many different competencies spread throughout higher education institutions.

Institutional and library strategies

An important question is whether there are organizational and strategic preconditions that must be met in order to succeed. Those institutions advocating more active learning styles will benefit especially from increased cooperation. The pay-off for students is an increase in information literacy and critical thinking skills, core competencies for knowledge workers.

Even if there is no shared institutional vision on education, there is no excuse for librarians to wait and see. It just implies that they have to find alternative routes. One nice thing about networked organizations is that one can build them without the consent of administrators. With or without an institutional strategy, it is still a librarian's task to support teaching and learning, and to develop relationships with faculty further and in the direction of supporting their teaching.

Challenges for the Libraries

There is an evolving shared vision of the new information world. It is a world of ubiquitous, reasonably priced digital information in any and all media, available to everyone from a computer, television, palm, or wrist, as predictable, ordinary, and universal as a toaster.

In addition to traditional text-based information, data accessible through the digital library system will include non-text information (photographs, drawings, illustrations, works of art); streams of numeric data digitized sound and moving visual images; multi-dimensional representations of forms or data and the capacity to integrate these data into new representations drawn from many different sources.

Most important, the digital library system would be ever-changing, dynamic, and interactive, allowing users to engage together in collaborative investigations; empowering discussions between readers and authors; enabling open, public, democratic debate.

Unlike traditional libraries, digital libraries don't reside in a building: correctly designed, their information arrives as needed at the user's screen.

Building the National Information Infrastructure, and its constituent digital library system, is one of the pivotal challenges of this century. Many of the most difficult tasks are social and cultural, economic, and technical.

There are three problem areas in each of these domains. Each requires cooperation among many and varied groups; there are no obvious, easy solutions; and all must be addressed successfully in building a digital library system.

The real challenge consists of building and scaling large, distributed digital library networks, including thousands of libraries, each containing terabytes of data. But users don't want to have to know. The technical challenges are many and varied. Here are a few:

- How would these libraries talk to each other?
- How would a user (or a user's agent) know where to look for what?
- How could search results be sorted, selected, merged, and transmitted back to users?
- How would large, distributed systems learn and evolve?
- How could data integrity and security be ensured?
- How about attribution, authorization, and payment?

- How could misuse be detected and corrected?
- How could failures be contained and fixed?

Digital libraries will require more authorizations and more funds from more users to more rights holders than has ever been contemplated in a nondigital world. Rights and royalties management will need to link and authorize access to information in many different forms, created and distributed under diverse rights-owning systems (e.g., print, film, sound, photographs). Copyright owners will require assurances that users will not be allowed to create derivative works without permission or to disseminate the information beyond the bounds of the authorization. And owners and users will need evidence that the information sought, and subsequently provided, has not been accidentally or maliciously altered.

Users will be unwilling or unable, in many cases, to define precisely all the uses to be made of a document; indeed, the power of digital representations derives in part from their flexibility and potential for unanticipated, new, productive uses. No comprehensive digital library can succeed without these conditions being satisfied. The digital library system must include a copyright management system that:

- provides for confidential, automated rights and royalty exchange;
- ensures owners and users that information is protected from
- unauthorized, accidental, or intentional misattribution,
- alteration, or misuse;
- ensures rapid, seamless, efficient linking of requests to authorizations for information use; and
- encompasses effective billing and accounting mechanisms.

A huge amount of money is involved in digital libraries and more research is needed on each of the following topics.

cost of communications infrastructure

cost of computer infrastructure, and

cost of information

Estimates of the cost of a national fiber-optic network depend on whether the fiber is deployed to the "last mile" for local access. It's impossible now to calculate the cost of the new computer hardware and software needed to take advantage of the new capabilities because much of it doesn't exist yet. No one has yet effectively estimated what all the information stored in a comprehensive digital library system would be worth.

There are a number of proposals detailing who should pay for digital library development. These include everything, from providing regulatory incentives for the regional telephone operating companies and cable operators to accelerate their investment in the infrastructure, to federal support, to encouraging investment by local gas and electric utilities.

Social and cultural challenges also come in the way of developing a digital library system. Also there are legitimate concerns about the risks involved in management of the infrastructure. By some estimates, this would increase the cost of installing fiber by as much as 50 percent, as well as raise significant public policy questions.

5
Digital Library Resources and Projects

The recent advancements in science and technology have led to miraculous changes in the art of recording and reproduction of knowledge making it possible to preserve it with greater accuracy and durability at a cheaper cost. An unimaginably vast amount of information is stored and reproduced now with the help of electronic devices.

Digital libraries came into being as a result of technological advancements in the field of electronics engineering as well as the changing requirements and expectations from the traditional libraries. They are also referred as the collections of information stored in digital format and accessible over a communication network. Digital libraries, in fact revolutionized the process of collection, storage, management, accessibility and transmission of information without involving any constraints of space and time.

Digital libraries are increasingly being developed almost in every country of the world. They are the future avatars of the present day libraries. Most of them are in the process of making and are generally being developed in isolation by a number of organizations specially the educational institutions all over the world. Once developed and connected, the digital libraries will supercede all the traditional libraries of today reducing them to merely the museum of books. It is going to be happened within a short span of time since their vast capacity of accommodating resources, speed of information retrieval and accuracy in operations they offer is unparallel to the existing type of libraries.

A recent survey conducted by info/librarian.com enlists the following libraries being developed at the international level:

International Resources and Projects

* Alexandria Digital Library Project
  http://www.alexandria.ucsb.edu/
* California Digital Library
  http://californiadigitallibrary.org
* Collect Britain: Putting history in place
  http://www.collectbritain.co.uk/
* Colorado Digitization Programme
  http://www.cdpheritage.org/
* Cornell Library Historical Mathematical Monographs
  http://historical.library.cornell.edu.math/
* Digital Library for Earth System Education
  http://dlese.org/dds/index.jsp
* Digital Library of Historical Directories
  http://historicaldirectories.org/
* Digital South Asia Library
  http:dsal.uchicago.edu/
* eScholarship Editions
  http:texts.cdlib.org/scholarship/
* Ethnomathematics Digital Library
  http://www.ethnomath.org/
* History E-book Project
  http://historyebook.org/
* Informedia: Digital Video Library Project
  http://informedia.cs.cmu.edu/
* Inventory of Canadian Digital Initiatives
  http://www.nlc-bnc.ca/initiatives/erella

* Librarycompany.org
  http://www.librarycompany.org/
* Metaarchive.org
  http: / /www.metaarchive.org/ index.htm
* Mind Project
  http://www.mind-project.org/
* National Science Digital Library
  http: / / nsdl.org/
* NYPL Digital Libary
  http: / / digital.nypl.org/
* Open-Video-Project.org
  http: / /www..open-video.org/
* Networked Digital Library of Thesis and Dissertations [NDTLD]
  http: / /www.ndltd.rog/
* New Zealand Digital Library
  http://www.nzdl.org/cgi-bin/library
* Stanford Digital Library Project
  http: / /www-diglib.stanford.edu/
* UC Berkeley Digital Library Project
  http: / / elib.cs.berkeley.edu/
* Universal Library
  http://www.ulib.org/html/index.html/

The above libraries may be visited at the addresses given with them.

Indian Resources and Projects

The following digital library projects have been identified by infolibrarian .com in India.

* Digital Library of India
* Digital Libary of Indian Institute of Management, Kozhikode

* Digital Libary of Library and Information Science
* Indira Gandhi National Centre for the Arts [IGNCA] Digital Library
* Nalanda Digital Library
* Vidyanidhi: Digital Library and E-Scholarship Portal
* Archives of Indian Labour

Below, we will discuss some of the most relevant of them in detail:

Digital Library of India

It is a digital library of books, which is free-to-read, searchable, predominantly in Indian languages, available to everyone over the Internet. Very soon it is expected that this portal would provide a gateway to Indian Digital Libraries in science, arts, culture, music, movies, traditional medicine, palm leaves and many more. This project is a collaboration between different Indian institutes and Universities and Carnegie Mellon University under Universal Digital Library Project.

The mission is to create a portal for the Digital Library of India which will foster creativity and free access to all human knowledge. As a first step in realizing this mission, it is proposed to create the Digital Library with a free-to-read, searchable collection of one million books, predominantly in Indian languages, available to everyone over the Internet. This portal will also become an aggregator of all the knowledge and digital contents created by other digital library initiatives in India. Very soon it is expected that this portal would provide a gateway to Indian Digital Libraries in science, arts, culture, music, movies, traditional medicine, palm leaves and many more. The result will be a unique resource accessible to anyone in the world 24x7, without regard to socioeconomic background or nationality.

One of the goals of the Digital Library of India is to provide support for full text indexing and searching based on OCR (optical character recognition) technologies where available. The availability of online search allows users to locate relevant information quickly and reliably thus enhancing student's success in their research endeavors. This 24x7 resource would also provide an excellent test bed for language processing research in areas such as machine translation, optical character recognition, summarization, speech and hand writing recognition, intelligent indexing, and information retrieval in Indian languages.

It is our expectation that the Digital Library of India will be mirrored at several locations worldwide so as to protect the integrity and availability of the data. The DLI will also partner with other country specific Digital Libraries initiatives as part of the Universal Library Project (www.ulib.org) spearheaded by Prof. Raj Reddy and Carnegie Mellon University.

The primary long-term objective is to capture all books in digital format. It is believed that such a task is impossible and could take hundreds of years, and never be completed. Thus, as a first step we are planning to demonstrate the feasibility by undertaking to digitize 1 million books (less than 1% of all books in all languages ever published) by 2005. We believe such a project has the potential to change how education is conducted in much of the world.

A secondary objective of this project will be to provide a test bed that will support other researchers who are working on improved scanning techniques, improved optical character recognition, and improved indexing. The corpus this project creates will be one to three orders of magnitude larger than any existing free resource.

The principal benefit of the Digital Library will be to supplement the formal education system by making knowledge available to anyone who can read and has access. Libraries have played a vital role in the advancement of human society. Societal advance depends on young people having access to books via libraries and other means. We expect that making this unique web resource available free to everyone around the world will enhance the learning process.

Libraries are unevenly distributed around the world and within each country. In the U.S., the NCES Survey noted that in 1996, 3,408 of 3,792 institutions of higher education had libraries holding 806.7 million volumes. The 112 largest university libraries in the United States and Canada each have at least 1.8 million books. They are members of the Association for Research Libraries. Massachusetts has about 25 million volumes; New York has about 31 million volumes, and California has about 40 million volumes in their ARL Libraries (Association for Research Libraries, 1999/2000). Other states, such as North and South Dakota , have no large libraries. A few large public libraries have several million volumes. However, most junior colleges, high schools, and public libraries have much smaller collections. Making this large knowledge repository can revolutionize research at all levels of education and give a much-needed boost at minimal cost to our national educational infrastructure. This impact will be further enhanced given the convenience of online access, and the benefit of full text searching at word and phrase levels.

A secondary benefit of online search is to make locating the relevant information inside of books far more reliable and much easier. Student success in finding exactly what they seek will increase and increased success will enhance student willingness to perform research using this large resource. NCES reports that 84 percent of libraries around the country are open between 60 and 80 hours a week. This digital library would be open all the 168 hours the week on a 24x7x365 basis. More than one individual will be able to use the same book at the same time. Thus, popular works will not be checked out and thus unavailable to others.

This million-book project will produce an extensive and rich testbed for use in further textual language processing research. It is hoped that at least 10,000 books among the million will be available in more than one language, providing a unique resource for example based machine translation.

Many believe that information is now doubling every two years. Machine summarization, intelligent indexing, and information mining are tools that will be needed for individuals to keep up in their discipline work, in their businesses, and in their personal interests. This large digitization project will enable extensive research in these areas.

Nalanda Digital Library

Nalanda is the result of the ongoing Digital Library nitiative at National Institute of Technology, Calicut Library. Nalanda Project aims at a full-fledged Digital Library at NITC to cater to the increasing demand for information resources from the Campus User Community as well as from Remote Users from rest of the Country. Some resources are open to all, otherwise they are resistricted to NITC campus and their recognised users. At present, it is in evolving stage.

NITC Library was started during 1963, with skeleton staff, inside NITC Campus with books as its major holding. During that period NITC was offering only Undergraduate Programs with a total strength of 180 students per batch.During 70's the Institute started Post-Graduate Programs in various disciplines and this led to the improvement in library facilities too. The Library started a separate Text Book Bank Section for the students during this period. Even though the effective area of the library remained same at 1340 sq.m, the holdings of the library increased substantially.

During 1980's, the student strength at NITC increased considerably both at Undergraduate and Post graduate level. NITC Library widened its operations in order to meet the consequent increased requirement for the library facilities.A separate section for weaker sections of the society(Scheduled Caste and ScheduledTribes)was introduced with the help of the State Welfare Board for SC/ST.Library also started subscribing to a number ofIndian and Foreign Journals to keep abreast with the technological and scientific developments in the world. The collection of the library also grew about three times its level during 1970's. The National Institute of Technology, Calicut, like many other Technical Institutions in the country, witnessed fast growth during the last decade due to the increased emphasis placed by the Govt. of India on higher education in Science and Technology. The intake of students increased in Undergraduate programs and 3 new UG programs in Computer Science & Engineering Production Engineering and Management and Architectural Engineering were started during the period. The Post-Graduate programs also doubled to 6 from the 1980 level of 3 programs. In addition to these, NITC started a Master of Computer Applications (MCA) Program during 1988. All these developments saw more users for library and library holdings increased substantially during the period. The library also increased its floor area to almost double that of 1960 level.

The operations of the library increased manifold during 1990-97. The holdings of the library increased to double the level of 80's and the area of library also increased with the addition of a new block. The demand on library also increased during this period due to the increase in student strength. The Institute had started a number of part-time programs and short-term training and executive development programs, increasing demand on the services of library. Even though the number of journals decreased during this period, the expenditure on this head had increased considerably as the library started subscribing to a number of important international journals. A separate reference reading room for the benefit of the users was started during this period. Similarly a full-fledged D.T.P centre with a graphics studio to meet the publishing needs of the Institute, and a separate Xerox centre were started during this period. A video section with more than 100 titles was started during this period in order to improve the learning resource collection. The services of the library to the weaker sections of the society also increased substantially. The holdings of books reserved separately for the use of students belonging to SC/ST communities had increased during this period.

Digital Library of Indian Institute of Management, Kozhikode

This digital library developed by IIMK library holds documents on management, economics, sociology, etc and IIMK staff publications. The number of documents included are less as the library is in development stage.

The Indian Institute of Management Kozhikode, IIMK is the fifth Indian Institute of Management. Established in 1996 by the Government of India in collaboration with the Government of Kerala, it provides education, training, consulting and research facilities in management.

Established in 1996 by the Government of India in collaboration with the Government of Kerala, it aims to provide education, training, consulting and research facilities in management. It is a Central Autonomous Body registered under the Societies Registration Act XXI of 1860, and is managed by a Board of Governors. The Director is the Chief Executive Officer of the Institute.

IIMK is located at Kozhikode, in south western India, a location made famous by the entry ofVasco Da Gama to India. The Institute operates from it's own, newly constructed campus, in the scenic ambience of approximately 100 acres in the Kunnamangalam locality of Kozhikode.

Indian Institute of Management Kozhikode seeks to achieve excellence and a leadership position in management education.

It aspires to :

* inculcate a spirit of life long learning
* strengthen capabilities of integrating concepts with applications and values
* contribute towards the development of communities of dependable, capable, caring and fair minded individuals.

IIMK is dedicated to offering world class programmes in management education. Its academic programmes encompass a range of long term full time diploma programmes such as the Post Graduate Programme in Management, and a number of short duration executive education programmes

The Institute seeks to achieve excellence and a leadership position in management education and to become a major learning resource centre in the Asia-Pacific region.

The Institute seeks to inculcate a spirit of lifelong learning. It aspires to strengthen the capabilities of integrating concepts with applications and values. It aims to contribute towards the development of communities of dependable, capable, caring and fair-minded people.

The Institute's activities presently include teaching, research and consulting. The Major programmes and activities of the Institute are:

* Post Graduate Programme in Management
* Management Development Programmes
* Research
* Consultancy Services
* Seminars and Workshops

Digital libraries are now being developed almost in all the countries and in about each disciplines of study. India has no dearth of technical man power and it is hoped that the digital libraries will soon appear and consolidate their information resources for education and research activities.

6
Universal Digital Library

Universal Digital Library is a project proposal under the Indo-US Science and Technology Collaboration initiatives. It is intended to develop a digital library containing on million books and to make the same available for the mankind on the World Wide Web.

The aim of the project is to digitize around a million books in the next three years. This joint initiative is planned to synergetically capitalize on the availability of the state-of-the-art of hardware and software in the US for digitizing, storing and accessing of information and the quality manpower available in India. This would act as a forerunner for many such initiatives with other countries, particularly in China and Korea and would culminate in the grandiose vision of digitizing all the formal knowledge and make available in a location and time independent way for the benefit of the mankind.

Today's scanning technology offers the possibility of digitizing an entire book in two hours. In order to take million books to the web, it is estimated that around 1000 man years would be needed. If the project is carried out in a developed country like the United States of America, it would cost at least around 40M $ besides the cost of the hardware, space and energy. It is economically feasible to try this out in developing nations like India.

As part of this project, it is planned to create 10 centres across India that would be commissioned to run three shifts with a work force of 40 in each centre. This would be adequate to meet the manpower demand of 1000 man years in 3 years. Each centre would then require around 15 scanning stations (Total 150 Scanning Stations). The cost of each scanning station including its maintenance over the three years period would be approximately US $ 30,000. Thus with a hardware and software cost of 5M $, over the three years period, it looks plausible to think in terms of the Universal Digital Library that will hold at least a million books.

It is proposed that the hardware and software costs are met from the US side while the manpower needs are met by the Indian side.

Copyright Laws

Currently, the copyright laws do not permit books published in the last 50 years in India and 100 years in the US to be digitized and distributed free. These laws are based on the eariier era wherein the life cycle of Information products was large. Currently, obsolescence is the common thing in science and technology and in many areas the obsolescence rate is so rapid that the life cycle of Information products such as books is reduced to a few years. There is a world wide awareness of this and WIPO is seriously directing its efforts towards this issue. Indo-US team could generate critical inputs to shape the copyright laws world over in general and in India and the USA in particular, that would be in tune with the aspirations of the Digital Economy. This would also ensure that the copyright laws protect the interest of the creator and consumer of information and still make economic sense.

Further, it is proposed that most of the books, in the 'million books to the web' project would come from the United States. After scanning, modality could be worked out by which the books may be retained in the respective retained Centres. The latter may be justified by the fact that the cost of the transportation back to the US after digitizing may be high.

Research and Development

Several attendant technologies are to be developed besides the hardware and software and the identification of books for scanning in order to ensure that the books of Indian Origin are included dominantly in the digitization. First is the research and development needed to ensure that an error free character recognizer in Indian Languages is made available to the centres. Further, an appropriate software to identify various fonts and the title, heading etc and to create meta files that can be used for accessing the information has to be perfected. Most of the Indian knowledge particularly in Sanskrit etc may not be available in printed form at all and even if unavailable, the quality of the paper and the background may not be suitable for feeder based scanner and character recognizer. In such cases, appropriate speech technologies to convert speech to text in Indian Languages and / or photographic scanner technologies may have to be developed.

The technology development described above would also form the focus of the R&D efforts proposed under the Indo-US collaboration. On the Indian side, the Indian Institute of Science, Bangalore would act as a nodal agency to coordinate amongst various academic institutions and governmental agencies from the Indian side. The Carnegie Mellon University would play the same role from the US side.

Vision

For the first time in history, all the significant literary, artistic, and scientific works of mankind can be digitally preserved and made freely available, in every corner of the world, for our education, study, and appreciation and that of all our future generations.

Up until now, the transmission of our cultural heritage has depended on limited numbers of copies in fragile media. The fires of Alexandria irrevocably severed our access to any of the works of the ancients. In a thousand years, only a few of the paper documents we have today will survive the ravages of deterioration, loss, and outright destruction. With no more than 10 million unique book and document editions before the year 1900, and perhaps 100 million since the beginning of recorded history, the task of preservation is much larger. With new digital technology, though, this task is within the reach of a single concerted effort for the public good, and this effort can be distributed to libraries, museums, and other groups in all countries.

Existing archives of paper have many shortcomings. Many other works still in existence today are rare, and only accessible to a small population of scholars and collectors at specific geographic locations. A single wanton act of destruction can destroy an entire line of heritage. Furthermore, contrary to the popular beliefs, the libraries, museums, and publishers do not routinely maintain broadly comprehensive archives of the considered works of man. No one can afford to do this, unless the archive is digital.

Digital technology can make the works of man permanently accessible to the billions of people all over the world. Andrew Carnegie and other great philanthropists in past centuries have recognized the great potential of public libraries to improve the quality of life and provide opportunity the citizenry. A universal digital library, widely available through free access on the Internet, will improve the global society in ways beyond measurement. The Internet can house a Universal Library that is free to the people.

Mission

The mission is to create a Universal Library which will foster creativity and free access to all human knowledge. As a first step in realizing this mission, it is proposed to create the Universal Library with a free-to-read, searchable collection of one million books, primarily in the English language, available to everyone over the Internet. Within 10 years, it is expected that the collection will grow to 10 Million books. The result will be a unique resource accessible to anyone in the world 24x7, without regard to nationality or socioeconomic background.

The first major project of Universal Library is the Million Book Digital Library project. Typical large high-school libraries house fewer than 30,000 volumes. Most libraries in the world have less than a million volumes. The total number of different titles indexed in OCLC's WorldCat is about 48 million. One million books, therefore, is more than the holdings of most high-schools, and is equivalent to the libraries at many universities and represents a useful fraction of all available books.

One of the goals of the Universal Library is to provide support for full text indexing and searching based on OCR (optical character recognition) technologies where available. The availability of online search allows users to locate relevant information quickly and reliably thus enhancing student's success in their research endeavors. This 24x7 resource would also provide an excellent testbed for language processing research in areas such as machine translation, summarization, intelligent indexing, and information retrieval.

The Universal Library will be mirrored at several locations worldwide so as to protect the integrity and availability of the data. Several models for sustainability are being explored. Usability studies would also be conducted to ensure that the materials are easy to locate, navigate, and use. Appropriate metadata for navigation and management would also be created.

The primary long-term objective is to capture all books in digital format. It is believed that such a task is impossible and could take hundreds of years, and never be completed. Thus, as a first step it is planned to demonstrate the feasibility by undertaking to digitize 1 million books (less than 1% of all books in all languages ever published) by 2005. Such a project has the potential to change how education is conducted in much of the world.

A secondary objective of this project will be to provide a test bed that will support other researchers who are working on improved scanning techniques, improved optical character recognition, and improved indexing. The corpus this project creates will be one to three orders of magnitude larger than any existing free resource.

Technical Details

1. Database creation

Creating a scalable database to support the Universal Library is one of the desired objectives. The resulting globally distributed database will appear to be a virtual central database from any place around the world. Mirroring the database in several countries will also ensure security and availability. The database will house both an image file and a text file at about 50-60 megabytes per book. A 100 terabytes of online storage currently costs around $150,000 and is expected to be under $5000 by year 2005 and thus making it possible to mirror the site in many countries.

2. Scanning

Earlier in the project, the scanner of choice was an inexpensive duplex scanner that required the books to be disbound so that the pages could be fed through in batches. While the economy and speed of this technique were most attractive, several technical problems occurred. The pages had to be cut on all four edges for smooth feeding. The project required the purchase of a $10,000 guillotine to accomplish this. The guillotine was somewhat dangerous, required in-depth training in use and safety, slowed the process, and nullified the economy of the inexpensive scanner.

Dust, an inevitable accompaniment to older books, proved to be a formidable opponent. Dust caused frequent jamming and subsequent cleaning of the scanner. Paper fixatives were employed to counteract the dust. Spraying on the fixative slowed the project and was not entirely satisfactory.

Currently, the Universal Library project uses a Minolta PS7000 overhead scanner, which is potentially able to scan 10000 pages operating on a 3-shift basis. Although this scanner was 5 times more expensive than the conventional roll-fed double sided scanner we used earlier, it proved to be more reliable. Books did not have to be disbound. The image processing software for curvature correction, deskewing, despeckling and cropping allows for thick books to be scanned either flat or in an angled cradle that reduces wear on the spine. Careful training is required to operate the scanner, and several different employees were successfully trained in our pilot experiment.

In summary, the advantages of the Minolta scanner were:

* Disbinding via a guillotine is not necessary.
* Books can be reused in their original form.
* Dust, thick paper, and long books can be easily accommodated.
* Training requirements are reasonable.
* Equipment is reliable

3. Data Production

The current approach for document scanning is to digitize the documents at the archival quality of 600 dots per inch (dpi) as a binary image (1 bit per pixel). The resulting images are stored as TIFF (Tagged Image File Format) files. (TIFF version 5.0 is acceptable. Subject to testing, version 6.0 (or later) may also be acceptable). The resolution of the images is high enough so as to permit reading of the the original pages directly on a computer screen.

4. Optical Character Recognition (OCR)

We do not plan to correct the OCR output as part of this project. The primary function of OCR is to allow searching inside the text. Unlike in other efforts, the output of the OCR text will not be used for direct viewing by the public. It will only be used for creating a searchable index (where errors tend to have limited impact).

Because words are often repeated, the 98% success rate will allow students and scholars to find relevant passage. In the pilot projects, the OCR program Abby Fine Reader was run after the scanning was completed.

Chinese and Japanese OCR programs are also available

and will be used whenever needed. This project has also stimulated efforts towards the development of OCRs in Indian Languages. Providing a testbed that will allow for the creation of even better OCR programs is one of the goals of this project. Scholars will be able to run newer OCR programs over the scans and possibly correct the output manually.

5. Metadata

Digital Library Federation standards and metadata best practices will be used throughout this project. Bibliographic metadata for the pilot project will be derived from existing library catalog records. Carnegie Mellon libraries developed software that uses the standard Z39.50 protocol to search and retrieve relevant metadata from catalog records fields. Thus, author, title, and publication data do not have to be rekeyed.

Entering metadata information manually is time-consuming. One of the current research projects is the creation of software for "automatic discovery of document structure". This will permit users to create hyperlinks which are not present in the original printed version of the book and navigate through the chapters.

Administrative metadata supports the maintenance and archiving of the paper or digital objects and ensures their long-term availability by providing information about how the files were created and stored. Administrative metadata will be maintained internally as file descriptions in the project databases and externally as part of the copyright permission database.

The Digital Library Federation, a supporter of this project, has several initiatives underway that will allow commercial browsers to harvest metadata more aggressively. The results of DLF's metadata harvesting project will be explored for possible application to the resources produced in this project (www.diglib.org).

6. Quality control

The standards established for quality control are those

currently endorsed by the Digital Library Federation, whose missions include the establishment of best practices and the development of standards. The project must maintain a 98% accuracy rate for the quality of images and the inclusion of all pages.

The process of scanning a book involves finding a library that owns the book, pulling the book, transporting the book to the scanning site, scan the pages, and returning the book to the original library. This process will be expensive. Maintaining high quality the first time the book is scanned will be essential. A demonstration of high quality, reliable work done on materials currently in China and India will give U.S. libraries confidence that their collections should be shared.

Benefits

The principal benefit of the Universal Library will be to supplement the formal education system by making knowledge available to anyone who can read and has access. Libraries have played a vital role in the advancement of human society. Societal advance depends on young people having access to books via libraries and other means. Making this unique web resource available free to everyone around the world will enhance the learning process.

Libraries are unevenly distributed around the world and within each country. In the U.S., the NCES Survey noted that in 1996, 3,408 of 3,792 institutions of higher education had libraries holding 806.7 million volumes. The 112 largest university libraries in the United States and Canada each have at least 1.8 million books. They are members of the Association for Research Libraries. Massachusetts has about 25 million volumes; New York has about 31 million volumes, and California has about 40 million volumes in their ARL Libraries (Association for Research Libraries, 1999/2000). Other states, such as North and South Dakota, have no large libraries. A few large public libraries have several million volumes. However, most junior colleges, high schools, and public libraries have much smaller collections. Making this large knowledge repository can revolutionize research at all levels of education and give a much-needed boost at minimal cost to our national educational infrastructure. This impact will be further enhanced given the convenience of online access, and the benefit of full text searching at word and phrase levels.

A secondary benefit of online search is to make locating the relevant information inside of books far more reliable and much easier. Student success in finding exactly what they seek will increase and increased success will enhance student willingness to perform research using this large resource. NCES reports that 84 percent of libraries around the country are open between 60 and 80 hours a week. This digital library would be open all the 168 hours the week on a 24x7x365 basis. More than one individual will be able to use the same book at the same time. Thus, popular works will not be checked out and thus unavailable to others.

This million-book project will produce an extensive and rich testbed for use in further textual language processing research. It is hoped that at least 10,000 books among the million will be available in more than one language, providing a unique resource for example based machine translation.

Many believe that information is now doubling every two years. Machine summarization, intelligent indexing, and information mining are tools that will be needed for individuals to keep up in their discipline work, in their businesses, and in their personal interests. This large digitization project will enable extensive research in these areas.

Philosophy of Content Selection

The Million Book Project envisages to develop a collection of one million digital books by adopting a staged approach as described below. The Million Book project will adhere to the U.S. copyright law.

U.S. collections will primarily include the following types of materials:

1. Coordination of Selection

Creating one digital copy and mirroring it in different locations will suffice, and will support the multiple uses at any time. Preliminary discussions with OCLC as a host for a registry of scanned items are underway. Certain key projects, such as the Making of America project, are already represented in the OCLC database as digital books. Other large digitization projects may require some data entry of their content in order to avoid duplication.

2. Non-copyrighted materials

Materials published before 1920 are in the public domain and may be scanned for this project. Several large academic libraries are considering shipping materials from their repositories of little used books to India or China. These books will be scanned there and then returned to where they came from. To reduce the costs of selection, the project will probably develop a strategy of selecting key topics and then removing large runs of books and journals from a selected repository. Having a reasonable turn-around time will be essential to the success of the project. A strategy has been devised to understand the logistics of shipping the materials and the impact of their absence from the home library.

The 1909 copyright law granted copyright for 28 years. Rights holders could then renew the copyright for another 28 years; many publishers and authors did not exercise that renewal option. Thus, some books published after 1922 (56 years prior to the 1978 effective date of the 1976 act) may be out of copyright. In order to provide for the efficient checking of status of these books, the copyright renewal records for books for these years have been scanned and made available online at www.ulib.org. Similar records for other formats, such as serials and audiovisual material, will also be made available as a part of this resource.

Government documents are also in the public domain and may be included in this project. Many participating libraries are repositories for full runs of government documents and could supply them to the project, as could the Library of Congress. The inclusion of these documents will allow for more recent material to enter the project legally and to become available to a broader audience and in a more accessible manner. Many government documents are currently available in digital form. The creation of these back files would enhance those resources.

The Chinese delegation is most eager to have technical reports and science and technology dissertations as a part of this project. Scholars and universities producing these scientific material have copyright interests in them. Gaining university permission might be fairly straightforward. A good-faith attempt would also have to be made to obtain the permission of the scholars. That could be a part of an externally funded copyright clearance project, but no pilot-study has been made to allow for an estimate of contact rate and subsequent success. If some arrangement could be made with University Microfilms to scan dissertations of selected universities from microfilm, which would be cheaper and easier to transport, such an initiative might satisfy a strong desire among all participants to increase science content.

3. Copyrighted materials

The 1998 Copyright law grants copyright to authors for their lifetimes plus 70 years or for 95 years. Patent law, by contrast, gives 20 years. A.W. Mellon's JSTOR project developed the concept of a moving wall that allowed the inclusion of materials over five years old. Journal publishers generally agreed that the economic value of that material was greatly reduced and granted permission for its inclusion in this most successful project. A similar broad publisher agreement about the point at which economic value of a print book declines is greatly needed. Books often go out of print in two or three years but remain in copyright and thus be unavailable for over 90 years.

Dr. Raj Reddy and Dr. Peter Shane, Director of the Institute for the Study of Information, Technology and Society recently had a conversation with a major book publishers to explore the possibility of taking a broad publisher approach to receiving copyright permissions. Certain publishers, including the National Academy Press, have had the experience that when they digitized their books, sales increased because attention was focused on the material and the users were not yet ready to read the books online. Authors' guilds will also be contacted to see if they would be interested in granting permissions.

Three conditions seem to be necessary to attract publishers to the scanning of their out of print but in copyright titles:

* Publisher should receive a tax deduction for contributing the title to this project. The tax deduction might reflect revenues previously generated by the title.
* When a print on demand feature becomes a part of this project, publishers should collect royalties on books printed.
* If a book were to return to general popularity, as the effect of the movie Titanic had on the sales of out of print titles, the publisher should be able to withdraw the permission for a fee. The publisher might be expected to reimburse the project for the costs of digitizing the title and maintaining it online.

Dr. Michael Shamos, a Director of Carnegie Mellon's Universal Library project and an intellectual property attorney, recommends the following approach to copyright clearance: The million book project will make a good faith effort to clear copyright on appropriate materials by sending the publisher of record a letter asking for permission. Replies will be recorded in the administrative metadata. If the publisher has returned the rights to the author, the author will be contacted. Subsequent copyright holders will be contacted as needed.

4. Best books approach

The project will seek publisher permission to scan books from Books for College Libraries (BCL), one source for core academic books in English. A previous study done at Carnegie Mellon University Libraries indicates that 22% of publishers granted permission for scanning and mounting on the web. The materials in the study were a random sample of Carnegie Mellon Libraries' books and included a broad range of dates, publishers, and in and out of print status.. Numerous difficulties from out of business publishers, lack of publisher records, return of copyright to authors, and other circumstances were identified. Subsequently, Carol Hughes, the collections development officer for Questia, corroborated Carnegie Mellon's experience.

OCLC owns a database of books from the latest edition of Books for College Libraries. BCL contains about 50,000 titles. A 22% success rate in clearing copyright would result in 10,000 of the best books for college students being included in the project. Clearing copyright is labor intensive and expensive. Bradd Burningham's recent article estimated those costs ("Copyright Permissions" in Journal of Interlibrary Loan, Document Delivery, and Information Supply, 11:2 (2000), 95-111). The BCL database, however, will allow for sorting by publisher so that permission requests can contain the names of several books. A quick sample indicates that as many as 25,000 publishers may be represented there. Despite the expense, this commitment to quality should be attempted. Carnegie Mellon University Libraries will seek private foundation funding to undertake this project.

Publishers increasingly see that digital presentation of their works can attract buyers. They are interested in exploring ways in which their out of print titles may be returned to profitability. Continued work with publishers through the course of this project may attract many of them to it. That would be most beneficial in enriching the content to be made available.

Current Status

Now we will describe activities used to establish protocols, to select standards to be used, and to address issues of indexing and retrieval. Workflow and training programs to support the larger project are being developed. Both the content and the mechanisms for using it will be made available in open source code.

One of the key activities has been to work with libraries within United States who will participate in providing content for scanning for the Universal Library. Members of the U.S. Digital Library Federation met on November 15 and 16, 2001 to work out the logistics of selecting and transporting materials from U.S. collections. Participants included the executive director of DLF, representatives of the NSF, OCLC, the Center for Research Libraries, collection development officers, and other librarians from the Library of Congress, the University of Washington, the University of California Berkeley, Stanford University, University of Illinois, University of Chicago, Penn State University, and the University of Pittsburgh.

The collection development librarians discussed:

* Collection focus to achieve a consensus on how to select the million books to be digitized.
* Involvement of outside scholars in selection issues to consider how non-librarian scholars might participate in selection.
* Copyright considerations to consider seeking permission for a set of in copyright "best books", such as those in Books for College Libraries.
* Standards for the work to review the current Digital Library Federation standards with a view to rapid adoption.
* Registry issues to move forward with OCLC in establishing a registry for books selected.
* Methods of transport to consider alternative means of transport and return.

* Timing to weigh the advantages of air containers and sea containers.
* Level of participation to determine minimum levels for contributors to the project.
* Incentives for participation to establish means of recognition for contributions through screen display and copies of the archives.

The outcome of this meeting was a plan for the selection and transmission of almost a million books to China and India over a multi-year period and a plan for assessing the success of the project annually.

The National Science Foundation's 2000 ITR grant cycle provided $500,000 for equipment to begin a Million Book pilot project. That grant will allow the purchase of 18 Minolta scanners to be located in India and China. These scanners have already been deployed to begin the scanning process. Additional scanners from other donors have permitted increase in the number of scanners deployed in India and China.

Participation of China

In August of 2001, the Chinese University Presidents, a Ministry of Education officials, and Chinese Academy of Sciences leaders visited the U.S. to reach agreements and to form a steering committee. Dr. Michael Lesk and Dr. Stephen Griffin from NSF attended this meeting and also hosted the Chinese delegation at the National Science Foundation. Professor Pan Yunhe, President of Zhejiang University; Dr. Gao Wen, Deputy President of the Graduate School, Chinese Academy of Science; Professor Chi Huisheng, Vice President of Beijing University; Professor Hu Dongcheng, Vice President of Tsinghua University; Professor Xu Zhong, Vice President of Fudan University; Professor, Zhang Yibin, Assistant to the President, Nanjing University; Mr. Guo Xinli, Vice General Director, Ministry of Education of China; Mr. Chen Jianping,

Vice Director, State Planning Commission of China; and Dr. Ching-Chih Chen of Simmons College attended.

Indian Contribution

A delegation from India visited US in May of 2002. This includes officials from from the Central and State Governments in India, Presidents of Universities and leading academicians. The Indian team included Prof MGK Menon, Chairman, Council of IIIT-A and IIT-B, Mr Yashwant Bhave, Jt Secretary, Ministry of Communication and Information Technology, Dr. IV Subbarao, Secretary Education, Government of Andhra Pradesh, Dr P. Krishniah, Executive Officer of TTD, and Mr Ajay Sawhney, Special Secretary for IT, Government of Andhra Pradesh, Dr Om Vikas, Senior Director, and Dr Chaturvedi, Director, of the Ministry of Communication and Information Technlogy, Government of India, Mr Surendra Bagde, Joint CEO MIDC, Mumbai. Dr. N. Balakrishnan, Chairman of the Division of Information Sciences, Indian Institute of Science, Prof Ashok Kolaskar, Vice Chancellor, Pune University, Dr MD Tiwary, Director, IIITA, Dr. Thangraj, Principal, AKCE, Mr Shreedhar, Secretary, AKCE, Dr Vaidhyasubramanian, Dean, SASTRA, representing the academia.

The meeting at CMU reviewed the current status of the work in India and created plans for the Million Book project in India, including technological challenges, legal and copy right issues, selection of books, meta data standards, search engines and server management. It was concluded that one of the Central Government agencies will take ownership of the Million Book Initiative in India, and will form a consortium that will give large impetus to the Indian efforts in a coordinated way.

Logistic Challenges

Accessing, scanning and webhosting of a million books is a major logistical challenge. A million books can be expected to be about 300 to 500 million pages. Throughput of each Minolta PS7000 scanner is about 6,000 to 10,000 pages per day based on three-shift operation. Using a 100 scanners, and about a 1000 person workforce, we can expect to complete the task of scanning a million books in 500 working days, or roughly two years of three shift operation. Given the uncertainities of quality of workers, equipment failures and power failures, we anticipate the scanning to be completed in less than four year time frame. This website will provide a graphic visualization of the progress after full speed of operation.

Movement of books from U.S. to India and China

India and China have large academic libraries and will contain much of the material to be included as part of the Million Book project. Over 700 of these libraries are OCLC members whose holdings can be easily ascertained. Because the scanning centers can be established anywhere, It is planned to establish them close to the libraries so that the books can be transported with minimal difficulty. It may be feasible to locate some of the scanning centers within the academic libraries, space permitting.

The task of shipping materials from the U.S. to China and India has been examined. The current plan is to primarily use air containers rather than shipping containers so as to reduce the damage to books and time of absence of the books from their owning libraries.

The books can be packed at originating libraries in small vendor boxes. It may be desirable to shrink wrap the books to ensure their intact arrival. The basic cost of shipping per book is expected to be about one to two dollars per book. Some libraries may select some materials that do not need to be returned because they are in the process of being discarded, but the default will be that materials will return to their originating libraries.

The Center for Research Libraries is willing to supply some of its own books to the project. It might also serve as a collection place towards the end of the project when the quantity of material to be shipped falls below the whole container level.

Future Sustainability

Sustainability is a long-term issue for this project; further research will be done on developing economic models to support this major contribution to education. Partial answers to this significant challenge are discussed below. Three establishments have potential for offering a sustainable model for this project—the Library of Congress and similar national libraries, OCLC, and other commercial concerns.

The million-book project will be a public good and as such must have a suitable repository that will continue to make it available to the public at no charge. That responsibility belongs most clearly to the national library in each country. Having a network of national libraries mirroring the resource around the world would be an appropriate and desired outcome.

Library of Congress

In the United States, the Library of Congress whould be the natural choice to act as the repository of all knowledge, because the national interest is so clearly served. However, the Library of Congress is not the national library of the United States, although many people assume that it is. In the LOC's own words in its mission statement: "THE FIRST PRIORITY of the Library of Congress is to make knowledge and creativity available to the United States Congress." It is only a lesser goal to make knowledge available to the public, and that is why the million-book project had to be undertaken outside of the scope of LOC. LOC is also the guardian of the copyright office and is apparently unwilling and/or unable to digitize anything to which there might be a copyright claim.

In 2001, Congress appropriated 100 million dollars for Digital Preservation, contingent on LOC's raising of $75 million in matching resources. The law allows the acceptance of gifts in kind as a part of the matching funding. The possibility of pledging the million-book project to LOC as matching funding for the Digital Preservation initiative is being explored. Even if the value of the project were only assessed on its inputs (equipment and labor), the Million Book project represents a significant investment.

OCLC

Another alternative might be for OCLC to maintain a free version of the resource. OCLC is a non-profit organization whose member libraries are committed to enhancing access to information. OCLC might cover its costs by charging member libraries a small fee when the million-book project is accessed through the 48 million-title database. For the millions of OCLC users, that convenience would be worth a small payment in an already existing fee relationship. OCLC's recent strategic planning initiatives identified the addition of more full text to the database, exploring archiving responsibilities, and becoming more international as important thrusts. OCLC would also be able to cover partial costs through some of the strategies listed below for publishers.

Commercial alternatives

The marketplace for electronic books is chaotic at this moment. Questia, designed to be an online source with at least 50,000 of the best books with sophisticated software to support searching and the creation of footnotes, marketed itself directly to students at a $20-30 monthly fee. Although the project was well capitalized and attracted a great deal of media attention, its operations have been significantly scaled back over the past year. Librarians have long observed that charging for resources in the academic environment reduces use. Students' desire for the convenience of online information sends them to the web and to the much-used electronic resources of their own libraries. That love of convenience apparently does not extend to purchasing Questia under current pricing models.

During the same period, the company netLibrary has announced that it will provide new full textbooks online. NetLibrary marketed itself to libraries through consortia. Use of materials, thus, was at no direct cost to students and faculty. While students appreciated the convenience of being able to use the resource online, they had many complaints about its functionality—in particular they resented the fact that books could only be printed one page at a time and that books were unavailable if another individual were using them. The economic models behind netLibrary charges also seemed to reflect an adherence to those of paper books rather than recognizing the economies of digital materials. The assets of netLibrary have since been sold to OCLC.

At this time, the marketplace responses suggest that turning the million book project into a private, revenue-generating source would not offer a sustainable model. JSTOR, Project Muse, and other digital journal projects that offer online materials with superior functionality and sustainability continue to flourish.

Publishers

Another commercial alternative might revolve around relationships with publishers. As publishers find that making the book available increases sales, they might be willing to support the project. The Universal Library website would support "buy" buttons, in return for a small share of the revenues from print-on-demand sales of out of print materials.

People CMU

* Dr. Raj Reddy, Founder and Director of the Universal Digital Library (UDL)
* Dr. Michael Shamos, Director of UDL, Intellectual Property
* Dr. Jaime Carbonell, Director of UDL, Language Technologies
* Dr. Robert Thibadeau, Director of UDL, Privacy and Security
* Dr. Gloriana St. Clair, Director of UDL, University Librarian, Content Selection

* Others: Eric Burns, Madhavi Ganapathiraju, Krishna Konduru, Kishore Madhav, Gabrielle V. Michalek

US Advisors

* Dr. Ching-chih Chen, Co-Principal Investigator, China-US Million Book Project
* Dr. Daniel Greenstein, Executive Director of the Digital Library Federation
* Dr. Brewster Kahle, President, Internet Archive
* Dr. Victor Zue, Professor, LCS, MIT
* Dr. Michael Lesk, National Science Foundation
* Dr. Stephen Griffin, National Science Foundation

China

* Dr. Pan Yunhe, President of Zhejiang University
* Dr. Gao Wen, Deputy President of the Graduate School, Chinese Academy of Science
* Mr. Guo Xinli, Vice General Director, Ministry of Education of China
* Mr. Chen Jianping, Vice Director, State Planning Commission of China
* Dr. Chi Huisheng, Vice President of Beijing University
* Dr. Hu Dongcheng, Vice President of Tsinghua University
* Dr. Xu Zhong, Vice President of Fudan University
* Dr. Zhang Yibin, Assistant to the President, Nanjing University
* Others

India

* Prof. M G K Menon, Chairman, Council of Indian Institute of Information Technology, Allahabad and Indian Insitute of Technology-Bombay (Mumbai)
* Dr. N. Balakrishnan, Chairman, Division of Information Sciences, Indian Institute of Science

* Mr. Yashwant Bhave, Joint Secretary, Ministry of Communication and Information Technology
* Mr. Surendra Bagde, Joint CEO, Mumbai Industrial Development Corporation
* Dr. Chaturvedi, Director, Ministry of Communication and Information Technlogy, Govt. of India
* Dr. Ashok Kolaskar, Vice Chancellor, Pune University
* Dr. P. Krishniah, Executive Officer of Tirumala Tirupati Devasthanams
* Mr. Ajay Sawhney, Special Secretary for IT, Government of Andhra Pradesh
* Mr. Sridharan, Secretary, Arulmigu Kalasalingam College Of Engineering
* Dr. IV Subbarao, Secretary Education, Government of Andhra Pradesh
* Dr. Thangaraj, Principal, Arulmigu Kalasalingam College Of Engineering
* Dr. M D Tiwari, Director, Indian Institute of Information Technology, Allahabad
* Dr. Vaidhyasubramanian, Dean, Shanmugha Arts, Science, Technology & Research Academy
* Dr. Om Vikas, Senior Director, Ministry of Communication and Information Technlogy, Govt. of India
* Others: Kiran Kumar, S. Srinivas

Partners

China

* Beijing University
* Chinese Academy of Science
* Fudan University
* Ministry of Education of China
* Nanjing University

* State Planning Commission of China
* Tsinghua University
* Zhejiang University

India

* Arulmigu Kalasalingam College Of Engineering
* Goa University
* Indian Institute of Information Technology - Allahabad
* Indian Institute of Science
* International Institute of Information Technology - Hyderabad
* Shanmugha Arts Science, Technology & Research Academy
* Tirumala Tirupati Devasthanams
* Maharashtra Industrial Development Corporation
* University of Pune

Funding Sources

Funding for the Million Book Project is coming from multiple sources. National Science Foundation is providing funding for equipment, India and China are providing manpower resources for scanning, indexing and hosting, and various companies and foundations are providing partial support.

National Science Foundation is providing funding for Scanners, Computers, Servers, and Software. These resources from NSF are augmented by China and India who are providing the manpower, about 2,000 man years of effort each, over a five year period, as their contribution to this project. This represents a twenty-to-one relative contribution by China and India to this project. They will assist in the selection of documents, software development and in digitizing of the books. English language materials already resident in those countries would be scanned first, before books are shipped from the United States. Chinese and Indian language based books would also be scanned where such material is available free of copyright restrictions. U.S. libraries, primarily members of the Digital Library Federation, would ship materials as needed, to be scanned and returned.

Donations

Activities such as selection and acquisition of books, packing and shipping costs, and quality assurance of the content are unfunded, and would greatly benefit from your support.

Tax Deductible donations may be made payable to "Million Book DL Project, CMU", and mailed to:

University Librarian,

Carnegie Mellon University,

Pittsburgh PA 15213 USA.

The Knowledge Conservancy

The Knowledge Conservancy is being created as a complement to the Universal Library Project.

Knowledge Conservancy is expected to help in the following ways:

* Accepting undirected and directed gifts to digitize and make freely accessible the works of man. This includes gifts that guarantee specified numbers of books or specified collections under the rule that access is free to the people.
* Funding the digitization of works and the ongoing upgrading of the digital works to the public. This funding can be directed to ongoing or new digitization projects. In addition, the funding will support one central master registry site that other sites will mirror.
* Promoting awareness of these digital works, and their importance, to the public at large.
* Selection and digitization of works may be at the discretion of the Conservancy, the projects it funds, or its donors.

* For example, a donor might contribute money specifically for digitizing works in a particular subject area. Selection of works might also be made from lists drawn up by scholars, requests over the Internet, and books donated to the Conservancy.
* Coordinating the efforts of digitization efforts. The Knowledge conservancy maintains a database to keep track of all book editions, music editions, art, and motion pictures that have been digitized and whether they have free access. This includes the capabilities to
* determine through its catalog whether access to a known document is already available,
* claim to be digitizing a document within a certain time period,
* reference a document with a hyperlink that does not 'go bad,'
* reference the content of a document based on accepted practice in document tagging, and
* allow machine interpretation of copyright restrictions and other restrictions on access and use.

Supporting Knowledge Conservancy

The Knowledge Conservancy seeks donations and support from people and organizations wishing to help make the cultural treasures of the world available to all.

Tax Deductible donations may be made payable to "Knowledge Conservancy, CMU", and mailed to:

University Librarian,

Carnegie Mellon University,

Pittsburgh PA 15213 USA.

Rationale for the creation of Knowledge Conservancy

The mission of the Knowledge Conservancy is the preservation of the world's cultural, historical, and scientific works, and their free access to the world over the Internet.

Many projects are already underway to put works on-line for general reading, including projects like American Memory, Project Gutenberg, and the Universal Library. While these projects are making some headway at preserving the world's cultural heritage, they still face major obstacles:

* Digitization efforts are widespread but relatively small and too often associated with restricted access. Collection owners are not motivated to provide free access often through ignorance about available techniques for recovering costs.
* Funding for the digitization of information—and for its ongoing preservation, maintenance, and delivery, once digitized — is less than needed to make a large-scale digital library of millions of items available to the global public.
* There is no global organizations seeking only to provide coordination of digitization efforts, sharing of limited resources, and global public awareness.
* A large portion of the world's cultural heritage is copyrighted. Thus far, projects have largely avoided using copyrighted material, because of the difficulty of acquiring rights. Many works risk being lost in obscurity long before the copyright expires. The result is that important bodies of work may be unavailable in widely accessible for for a long time, and possibly forever.

The Knowledge Conservancy promotes the widespread duplication of digital collections at many sites, to increase accessibility and minimize the risk of single-point failure.

Conservancy policy is that a digital copyright may be retained by the collection owner but the conservancy will have a perpetual right to provide free viewing access to the material through its universal library. Furthermore, free viewing access will be automatically and perpetually granted to any site that agrees to the conditions of copyright and agrees to solely bear the cost of the mirroring. The copyright owner will always have a right to a link defined on any of his pages viewed, as will the Knowledge Conservancy.

The Knowledge Conservancy will actively support and endorse, but will not fund, money making activities around the material that is free to read. Examples include ordering copies of a book or manuscript, paying to print, paying for high fidelity access, ordering CD or DVD ROMs, ebook editions, selling supplementary materials, searching tools, indexing tools, multilingual tools, and portals that provide new media presentations of the material.

The Knowledge Conservancy will fund (a) digitizing a work and (b) providing metadata about a work including cataloging metadata, metadata about the structure of the content inside the work (e.g., chapters, stanzas, link maps for images), metadata that controls copyrights, and full text (symbolic) conversion. It will not fund, but will strongly endorse and otherwise support, interpretative efforts.

The conservancy is not a standards making organization, but will provide online cross-disciplinary support and assistance in order to improve quality in digitization, free-to-read presentations, and long-term preservation and migration of digital works. The conservancy may charge fees for this support or provide referrals to organizations that charge fees for such support.

Copyright Disclaimer

All the books available at the Universal Library are either out of copyright or permission to scan has been granted. If this is incorrect the offending content will be removed on receiving information from the aggrieved party.

Some Clarifications

Information storage and management

The MBP when completed will produce approximately 250 million pages or 500 billion characters of information. The storage requirements for the image files will be approximately 50 petabytes ? an order of magnitude larger than any publicly available information base. Creating and managing such a vast information base poses many technological challenges and provides a fertile test bed for innovative research in many areas (described below). The MBP is a multi-agency, multi-national effort that will require the database to be globally distributed. For location independent access, this globally distributed database should appear to be a virtual central database from any place around the world. Mirroring the database in several countries will ensure security and availability. The network speeds at the various nodes would be different. Research in distributed caching and active networks would be needed to ensure that the look and feel of the database is the same from any location.

Search engines

The search engines of today work on the principle of keyword matching and perform searches in one language at a time. With a large corpus of multilingual data provided by the MBP, along with multilingual summarization and translation tools, a well-directed research effort would be needed to ensure concept- and content-based retrieval of knowledge from across multilingual data.

Image processing

The accuracy of Optical Character Recognition (OCR), even in some of the most developed languages, is hindered by the bad quality of the images. This is particularly true for older books and those that use ancient fonts for which the OCR is not tuned. Even the very best OCR accuracy of the order of 98% may not be acceptable in some cases. In order to obtain an improved accuracy close to 100%, advanced image processing research that will perform recognition beyond the character level will be needed. With the availability of large test data from the MBP and the exponentially increasing computing power of the microprocessors, well-directed image processing research would lead to near perfect optical recognizers.

Optical Character Recognition (OCR) in non-Romanic languages

The MBP will have considerable content in many Indian and Chinese languages. The development of OCR in many of the Indian Languages is far more complicated. For example, some of the problems in the development of OCR for Indian languages are:

* There are1500 spoken Indian languages and 17 scripts.
* Unlike English, where the number of characters to be recognized is less than 100, Indian scripts have several hundred characters to be recognized.
* Non-uniformity in the spacing of the characters within a word because of the presence of Consonant Conjuncts (vowel + consonant) makes OCR more difficult. Also, the presence of Consonant Conjuncts results in improper line segmentation. Programs will have to do further processing to segment the lines.
* Consonants take modified shapes when attached with the vowels. Vowel modifiers can appear to the right, on the top or at the bottom of the base consonant. Such consonant-vowel combinations are called modified characters. In addition, two, three or four characters can combine to generate a new complex shapes called compound characters. These characters are very difficult for a machine to recognize.
* In scripts like Bangla and Devnagari, all the characters in a word are connected by a unique line called shirorekha (also called head line). In these scripts, character segmentation is especially difficult.
* In south Indian scripts, vowels occur only at the beginning of a word as against the vowels in Oriya, where they occur anywhere within a word. So, the language morphology for some groups of scripts is different from the others.
* There is no universally acceptable standard encoding

scheme for Indian scripts. This necessitates a scheme where the output labels from the OCR system can be mapped to the labels used by the typesetter through a mapping table.

Because of the non-availability of quality-segmented data, the recognition rate of the Indian language OCR cannot be pushed beyond 90% using character level recognition. To obtain a higher recognition rate, word level information in the form of dictionary has to be used. A word corpus is essential, but such a word corpus for most of the Indian scripts is not available today. The MBP will be able to provide this important missing piece. Once such data is available, it will be possible to use advances in image recognition to develop the OCR in Indian and other non-Romanic languages.

Copyright laws and digital rights management

In the new digital economy, providing democratic access to information while suitably and reasonably rewarding the innovator is possible. The largest repertoire of free software available on the web in many cases has been the outcome of state supported research. This free availability of software has in fact contributed to more developments and hence an exponential growth of knowledge. Even in literary and scholarly publications, authors have experienced increase sales of their work whenever they are made freely available on the web. This is in tune with observations in the new economy that the companies that make more and more of their software freely available on the web, have their market capitalization enhanced. The MBP, with its proposed plans to make a large knowledge base freely available, will provide useful statistics for testing many economic and sociological models.

Language processing

The MBP will produce an extensive and rich test bed for use in further textual language processing research. It is hoped that at least 10,000 books among the million will be available in more than one language, providing a key testing area for problems in example based machine translation. In the last stage of the project, books in multiple languages will be reviewed to ensure that this test bed feature is accomplished.

Many believe that knowledge is now doubling at the rate of every two to three years. Machine summarization, intelligent indexing, and information mining are tools that will be needed for individuals to keep up in their discipline work, in their businesses, and in their personal interests. This large digitization project will support research in these areas. This will be of greater significance for the Indian languages where new tools for summarization, grammar and spell checking, thesaurus and translation dictionaries need to be developed.

The data provided by the MBP with the right research inputs will facilitate the development of language- and location-independent intelligence amplifiers for furthering information creation.

Permission to digitize titles

The MBP approach is to request permission for a range of years, for example, everything published prior to 1990. A publisher could specify the cut-off year or, alternatively, specify the list of titles for which they grant non-exclusive permission to digitize in the MBP.

Value-added services

The MBP is not developing a for-profit system. All of the content will be available free-to-read on the Internet. Participating publishers will get copies of the digitized books and metadata, and can themselves provide or enable others to provide value-added services to access the digital books. Permission granted to the MBP is NON-exclusive.

Reading the case study of the National Academy Press's experience putting their books online free-to-read could facilitate understanding and appreciation of the benefits of this approach. The case study is available at: http://www.press.umich.edu/jep/04-04/pope.html (Journal of Electronic Publishing, Vol. 4, Issue 4, May 1999)

Participation in the Program

The National Academy Press has given us permission to digitize all of their books published prior to 1995 and negotiations are on with MIT Press.

Accuracy in Scanning

Carnegie Mellon has established a workflow (based on pilot ?100 book? and ?1000 book? projects) that includes steps to insure capture of high resolution images and essential metadata, post-processing to correct skewing and crop dark borders surrounding the page images, and OCRing to create searchable ASCII text with 98% accuracy.

Sscanning a title

We expect/hope to return TIFF images to the publisher in about three months from the time permission is granted, but the time will depend on how long it takes us to locate copies of the books (after permission to digitize them is granted) and how many books are included in the group.

Print-On-Demand (POD) standards of Replica and Lightning Source

The MBP follows the standards and best practices supported in ?A Framework of Guidance for Building Good Digital Collections? developed by the Institute for Museum and Library Services in 2001 and endorsed by the Digital Library Federation in 2002.

See:http://www.diglib.org/standards/imlsframe.htm, http://www.imls.gov/pubs/forumframework.htm

More specifically, our guidelines for data production (excerpted from the MBP NSF proposal and based on pilot projects) are:

* Bitonal images with a pixel depth of 1 bit-per-pixel scanned at a resolution of 600 dots per inch (DPI). Images will be stored as ?Intel? TIFF (Tagged Image File Format) files with the header content specified. The compression algorithm used is ITU (Formerly CCITT) Group 4.

* TIFF version 5.0 is acceptable. Subject to testing, version 6.0 (or later) may also be acceptable.
* The initial-capture system includes dynamic thresholding or a similar feature to capture variability of darkness in the imprint and possibly darker (e.g., foxed) backgrounds from decay. Images should be as readable as the original pages.
* Typical expected data will be provided for most TIFF tags (normally, the data supplied by software default settings). A specification for the TIFF header will be produced to include scanner technical information, filename, and other data, but to be in no way a burden on the production service.
* Images will be written in sequential order, with corresponding 8.3 filenames, e.g., 00000001.tif as the first image in volume sequence and 00000341.tif as 341st image in volume sequence.
* Volumes provided to the MBP will be assigned unique identifiers that conform to 8.3 format. The images will be in directories named with the corresponding identifier (e.g., the volume identified as akf3435.001 will have a directory with the same name, and 00000001.tif through 0000000N.tif files within that directory).
* Images and directories (as specified above) will be written to gold CD-ROM according to agreed upon specifications and using ISO9660 format.
* Skew will be within a specified range of degrees allowed.

Administration of the MBP

Neither the consortium nor participating publishers will have an administrative role in the MBP. Administrative responsibility for the MBP belongs to officials at participating universities.

At Carnegie Mellon, the administrative officials are:

Dr. Raj Reddy, University Professor, School of Computer Science

Dr. Gloriana St. Clair, University Librarian

Dr. Mark Kamlet, Provost

The establishment of the Universal Digital Library id going to set a landmark in the history of libraries and learning. If it goes well that is very much expected, the largest full text database of books will be made available that can be accessed from any corner of the world by an unlimited number of users simultaneously.

7
Oxford Digital Library

Oxford is a unique and historic institution. As the oldest English-speaking university in the world, it can lay claim to nine centuries of continuous existence. There is no clear date of foundation, but teaching existed at Oxford in some form in 1096 and developed rapidly from 1167, when Henry II banned English students from attending the University of Paris.

Oxford became a centre for lively controversy soon with scholars involved in religious and political disputes. John Wyclif, a 14th-century Master of Balliol, campaigned for a bible in the vernacular, against the wishes of the papacy. In 1530, Henry VIII forced the University to accept his divorce from Catherine of Aragon. During the Reformation in the 16th century, the Anglican churchmen Cranmer, Latimer and Ridley were tried for heresy and burnt at the stake in Oxford. The University was Royalist in the Civil War, and Charles I held a counter-Parliament in Convocation House.

In the late 17th century, the Oxford philosopher John Locke, suspected of treason, was forced to flee the country. The 18th century, when Oxford was said to have forsaken port for politics, was also an era of scientific discovery and religious revival. Edmund Halley, Professor of Geometry, predicted the return of the comet that bears his name; John and Charles Wesley's prayer meetings laid the foundations of the Methodist Society.

The University assumed a leading role in the Victorian era, especially in religious controversy. From 1833 onwards The Oxford Movement sought to revitalise the Catholic aspects of the Anglican Church. One of its leaders, John Henry Newman, became a Roman Catholic in 1845 and was later made a Cardinal. In 1860 the new University Museum was the scene of a famous debate between Thomas Huxley, champion of evolution, and Bishop Wilberforce. Frm 1878, academic halls were established for women, who became members of the University in 1920. Since 1974, all but one of Oxford's 39 colleges have changed their statutes to admit both men and women. St Hilda's remains the only women's college.

During the 20th century, Oxford added to its humanistic core a major new research capacity in the natural and applied sciences, including medicine. In so doing, it has enhanced and strengthened its traditional role as an international focus for learning and a forum for intellectual debate.

The Digital Library

The Oxford Digital Library (ODL) is a key-component of the e-strategy of Oxford University Library Services (OULS). It has been established to create the intellectual framework and to develop the technical infrastructure for an enhanced service, providing online access to the vast scholarly library collections of the University. ODL will have a major role in co-ordinating and stimulating digitization activities in the University.

Main tasks of the Oxford Digital Library include:

* Access to digital resources
* The central digital conversion of library holdings
* Developing and setting standards for ODL digital resources
* Providing robust and sustainable online access for digital resources
* Building a critical mass of high quality digital materials from the University's collections to serve scholarship, teaching, and learning by assisting scholars and students from the University and elsewhere in the pursuance of their work
* Administering the Development Fund to promote the creation of digital content

* Supporting scholarly and library activities in fundraising for further digitization activities
* Providing advice and consultancy services for digitization projects

ODL plays a key role in the development of the hybrid library which comprises the whole range of library materials in print, micro and electronic form (both genuine electronic and digital converted). Equally it will promote Oxford's digital library collections throughout the world supporting the international reputation of the University of Oxford and maintaining and developing its excellence.

Services

Oxford Digital Library is currently establishing a range of core services to support the creation of digital resources from Oxford University Libraries Services holdings. Services will include:

* A central digital image capture service for the whole range of still images (black & white/bitonal, greyscale and colour).
* Advice and consultancy on key aspects of digital library developments and production, including digitization, metadata, storage, online delivery, workflow management, grant writing and costing
* A robust and flexible Digital Library system to ensure integrated access and sustainability for digital resources (currently under development).
* Providing reliable storage and archiving mechanism for OULS digital library projects in cooperation with Oxford University Computing Services (OUCS)
* Evaluation, development and provision of tools (i.e. image enhancement and OCR programs, XML-editors) to capture different kinds of data during the digital production process
* Linking to relevant resources for digital library development and repositories

ODL is required to evaluate and implement internationally agreed standards for digital library elements (i.e. technical parameters for image capture, metadata schemes and delivery protocols).

Digital Collections

Oxford University is internationally renowned for its scholarly library collections, and in particular for those of the Bodleian Library which has been a library of deposit for almost 400 years. The University has a long tradition in digital scholarship and there are a number of completed library projects focusing on the digitization of primary resources.

Although these collections are widely used, there is a clear demand for a closer integration of discrete collections of this kind. The ODL aims to offer a Digital Library architecture which will allow centralized access to digital resources, both those it creates itself and those acquired from outside. The use of established standards for descriptive metadata (i.e. EAD, TEI) is a precondition for this integration process. Existing digital library collections may be transferred step by step into a common architecture with an integrated retrieval mechanism.

Development Fund

The Development Fund (DF) of the Oxford Digital Library is a grant program with the overarching remit to enrich Oxford's library collections with a significant set of digital resources. It comprises a generous grant awarded by the Andrew W. Mellon Foundation to Oxford University to fund the essential infrastructure of ODL (equipment and staff) and to support a range of digital projects based on core research material from OULS holdings.

The grant programme for projects is managed by the Oxford Digital Library in collaboration with an Editorial Board, comprising scholars and librarians from within and outside Oxford.

During the initial development period, ODL DF funding for projects is anticipated to be in the region of £265,000. Only a limited number of projects can be funded at this stage. However, in addition to major digitization projects, a number of small-scale pilot projects focusing on new digital technologies or special conversion requirements will also be considered.

In accordance with the conditions of the Mellon grant, the use of materials from libraries within Oxford University Library Services will be a mandatory requirement for any proposal.

Previous calls for proposals were launched in October 2001 and March 2003. These calls invited project proposals from scholars in partnership with OULS libraries. It aims to promote scholarly effort with relevance to research and teaching by digitizing, delivering and enhancing major library holdings of Oxford University.

Principles and Guidelines

The Oxford Digital Library plans to build up a significant set of digital resources for local and remote online access. Like traditional collection development long-term sustainability and permanent availability are major goals for the Oxford Digital Library. Therefore the use of standards in the digital conversion process and for the description of digital resources will be essential for projects funded through and supported by ODL.

With respect to the overarching remit of ODL as a "Hybrid Library" digital resources provided by ODL will have to be compatible with that used in traditional libraries, at least to the extent of allowing integrated searching across distributed repositories.

The Oxford Digital Library provides technical expertise and experience for digital projects over the planning process and offers advice throughout the entire project process. Guidelines have already been published for best practices in metadata schemes; future guidelines will cover the digital conversion process, and metadata capture.

8
California Digital Library

The California Digital Library is the University of California's 11th University library. It was established in 1997 by University of California President Emeritus Richard Atkinson to build the University's digital library, assist campus libraries with sharing their resources and holdings more effectively, and provide leadership in applying technology to the development of library collections and services. Organizationally housed under the UC Office of the President, the CDL operates in close collaboration with all UC campuses and their libraries.

The mission of the Library is to harness technology and innovation, and leveraging the intellectual and cultural resources of the UC, the CDL supports the assembly and creative use of the world's scholarship and knowledge for the UC libraries and the communities they serve.

To achieve its mission, the CDL utilizes strategic partnerships and technical innovation to:

* Focus on digital library collections by investing in the means of developing, acquiring access to, and persistently managing digital collections.
* Invest in applications that help campus libraries and others build meaningful, cost effective, and customized services for the use of the University's scholarly, cultural, and learning resources.
* Provide collaborative leadership in the development of new forms of scholarly communication.
* Leverage its investments to influence the marketplace for scholarly information in the interest of the University, its libraries, and the communities they serve.

Organization

Harnessing technology and innovation, and leveraging the intellectual and cultural resources of the University of California, the California Digital Library supports the assembly and creative use of the world's scholarship and knowledge for the UC libraries and the communities they serve. Established in 1997 as a UC library, the CDL has become one of the largest digital libraries in the world.

The California Digital Library is housed under the University of California Office of the President, and is directed by Daniel Greenstein, the University Librarian for Systemwide Library Planning and the CDL. UC library groups, CDL advisory groups, CDL staff, and third-party partners all contribute to the workings of the CDL. Because the CDL is one of the UC libraries, it participates in systemwide library groups. CDL advisory and working groups provide guidance for specific CDL programs and initiatives.

The CDL staff support the CDL's mission and programs. Many staff members also serve on advisory committees and working groups focusing on the development of digital libraries.

CDL staff departments include:

* Administration
* Built Content
* Business Development
* Communication
* Digital Library Services
* Digital Library Technologies
* Digital Preservation Programs
* Office of Scholarly Communication

Collections & Services

With more than 32 million items in their collective holdings, the UC libraries make up the largest university research library in the world. The Library provides access to scholarly materials, databases of journal article abstracts and citations, electronic journals, publishing tools, and reference databases for the University of California community.

The CDL also builds collections and provides public access to cultural heritage materials though a variety of innovative programs such as Counting California, which hosts digital government information, and the eScholarship program, which assists in the creation and dissemination of UC-produced scholarship.

In addition, the CDL pursues technological innovations that enhance services for accessing, sharing, manipulating, and integrating scholarly content in all forms.

CDL collections and services include:

* **CaliforniaDigitalLibrary.org:** Provides a single point of access for the publicly available digital collections produced or managed by the UC.
* **CDL Image Demonstrator:** Allows users to search and view a collection of art and architecture images drawn from museum and art collections.
* **Counting California:** Offers "one-stop shopping" for government data and statistics about California.
* **Digital Preservation Program:** The CDL hosts the UC libraries' digital preservation program to ensure long-term availability and access to digital content.
* **Directory of CDL-Licensed Content:** Lists the CDL's extensive collections of digital resources, including article databases, electronic journals, and reference texts.
* **eScholarship Editions:** Provides access to digital texts and monographs, including more than 1,400 UC Press titles. A significant number of the electronic books are available for free to the public.
* **eScholarship Publications:** Showcases publications

from the eScholarship program, including interactive publications from the Electronic Cultural Atlas Initiative, legacy online journals such as the Dermatology Online Journal, and monographs from the UC International and Area Studies Digital Collection.

* **eScholarship Repository:** This free, open-access repository infrastructure supports the full range of scholarly output, from pre-publication materials to journals and peer-reviewed series, by offering UC departments direct control of publishing.
* **Melvyl Catalog:** A searchable catalog of library materials from the 10 UC campuses, the California State Library, the California Academy of Sciences, the California Historical Society, the Center for Research Libraries, the Giannini Foundation of Agricultural Economics Library, the Graduate Theological Union, the Hastings College of the Law Library, and the Lawrence Berkeley National Laboratory Library.
* **Online Archive of California (OAC):** Federates collections of digital materials (such as manuscripts, photographs, and art) held in the libraries, museums, and archives across California through a searchable database.
* **Request:** Enables UC faculty, students, and staff to enter requests from the Melvyl Catalog and journal article databases for materials. Items not available at a user's home campus are delivered via interlibrary loan, while items available at a user's home campus are delivered through the document delivery service.
* **SearchLight:** Allows simultaneous searches across multiple journal databases, book catalogs, and other information sources available through the CDL and the UC campuses.
* **UC-eLinks:** Provides a way to easily move from an article or book citation in an article database to the full online

content of the item, or, for print materials, to automatically look for a UC library location of the item.

Programs

The California Digital Library supports the assembly and creative use of the world's scholarship and knowledge for the University of California libraries and the communities they serve. To accomplish these goals, the CDL partners with the UC libraries, publishers, and other institutions in broad-based programs and initiatives. Programs host specific digital collections and services.

The CDL's programs include:

* **Collections:** Acquiring scholarly content, hosting digitized materials from UC collections and non-UC library and museum partners, and enabling the publication of original scholarly materials.
* **Services:** Enhancing services for discovering, sharing, manipulating, and integrating scholarly content.
* **eScholarship:** Fostering innovation and faculty experimentation in digital scholarly communication.
* **Digital Preservation:** Focusing on the persistent management of digital information.
* **Education, Communication, and Assessment:** Furthering the understanding of digital library products and the digital library domain; discovering needs, testing usability, and evaluating the use and usefulness of digital collections and services.
* **CDL Technologies:** Supporting the UC campus libraries and others in the application of technology for the development of scholarly digital collections and services.

Collections

The University of California's scholars and students conduct their research and learning while drawing from a significant portion of the world's knowledge held in the UC's library collections. Those collections grow and become more convenient to use through the California Digital Library's program to acquire and host scholarly materials in digital form.

The CDL leads a large collaborative effort to license electronic scholarly materials on behalf of the UC, in co-investment with the campus libraries. In addition, CDL hosts digital content created by the UC libraries and California partners, and makes these materials available for public use.

The CDL:

* Provides the UC community with more digital material than is available at any other university, including more than 8,000 electronic journals, tens of thousands of electronic books, and more than 250 article and reference databases.
* Saves millions of dollars compared to what would be spent by the campuses acting independently.
* Allows campus libraries to focus on local research and curriculum by economizing on costs for commonly needed materials and acquisition processes.
* Provides a deep and broad collection of online cultural heritage materials from UC and California libraries, museums, and historical societies via the Online Archive of California (OAC).
* Enables the experimental publication of scholarly output in open-access repositories.
* Encourages interactive use of government and social science statistics and data via Counting California.
* Forges partnerships with university presses and societies to digitally publish scholarly works.

New activities and explorations are focusing on:

* Publishing scholarly monographs in XML.
* Hosting digital image collections managed by UC Visual Resource curators.
* Providing access to local history collections.

* Cultivating the interchange of California's botanical information resources.

Services

Services allow scholars and students to search for and use items in the University of California collections and elsewhere. Services are the necessary complement to collections and to the activities of acquiring, managing, and preserving scholarly materials.

The California Digital Library pursues technological innovations that provide solutions to the UC libraries for the discovery, integration, manipulation, and sharing of scholarly content in all forms. The CDL provides some direct online services and makes tools available to the UC libraries and others for the customization of local services.

The digital services program relies on systemwide collaboration to identify, build, and implement services and tools that benefit the UC libraries and other partners.

Existing services, tools, and activities concentrate on:

* Discovering print and digital materials in the UC libraries and beyond, including the 32 million items in the UC libraries via the Melvyl® Catalog, and the large collections of cultural heritage materials from more than 70 California libraries and institutions in the Online Archive of California (OAC).
* Streamlining access to online and print materials by linking from article citations to the full online content or to the locations for printed materials via UC-eLinks.
* Manipulating content by providing tools to export citations to citation management software, or to create and export presentations using digital images.
* Creating and sharing scholarship by providing faculty with experimental publishing tools and infrastructure.
* Influencing commercial products by developing high-performance technical and functional requirements,

and by working with UC subject specialist librarians, known as Resource Liaisons, who monitor and influence licensed products.

* Supporting UC librarians by communicating with the Users Council, sponsoring workshops, and providing a Help Desk and guides for troubleshooting.

New activities and explorations are focusing on:

* Digital image services, with tools designed for classroom instruction.
* Federated searching or portal tools for the discovery and integration of disparate collections.
* Instructional technologies that integrate digital materials into learning and course management systems.
* Delivery of digital books to classrooms, labs, libraries, and individual readers.

EScholarship

Scholarly communication is the foundation of all academic activities. The traditional model of scholarly communication is based on journal publications, and in the current age, it has become expensive, restrictive, and increasingly limited in its ability to make information accessible. To address these concerns, the eScholarship program was initiated by the California Digital Library at the University of California.

The eScholarship program facilitates innovation and supports experimentation in the production and dissemination of scholarship. Through the use of innovative technology, the program seeks to develop a financially sustainable model and improve all areas of scholarly communication, including its creation, peer review, management, dissemination, and preservation.

New modes of scholarly publication include:

* Repositories for research and scholarly output, including

pre-publication materials and peer-reviewed content.

* Web-based publications of digitally reformatted content.
* Electronic editions of academic monographs of interest to both scholarly and general-interest readers.

In partnership with librarians, scholars, publishers, information technologists, and professionals in other memory organizations, the eScholarship program has developed several key collections and services:

* **eScholarship Editions:** Provides access to a growing collection of digital texts and monographs, including more than 1,400 UC Press titles. A significant number of the electronic books are available for free to the public.
* **eScholarship Publications:** Publications from the eScholarship program, including monographs from the UC International and Area Studies Digital Collection, journals and peer-reviewed series in the eScholarship Repository, experimental interactive publications like ECAI, and legacy content like the DOJ.
* **eScholarship Repository:** This free, open-access repository infrastructure supports the full range of scholarly output, from pre-publication materials to journals and peer-reviewed series, by offering UC departments direct control of publishing.

Digital Preservation

The University of California libraries are committed to maintaining world-class collections of scholarly information. To this end, essential information resources must remain available and accessible into the future—a growing challenge in the days of digital resources that are increasingly ephemeral and at risk.

In partnership with the UC libraries, the California Digital Library established the digital preservation program to ensure long-term access to the digital information that supports and results from research, teaching, and learning at UC. Included are ejournals, web-based content, digitally reformatted materials from UC libraries and museums, and online teaching and learning materials.

A priority of the digital preservation program is creating a preservation infrastructure composed of tools, guidelines, and best practices. This infrastructure will support independent preservation efforts throughout the University, helping meet UC's needs for the reliable archiving, management, and retrieval of digital information.

Other digital preservation activities include:

* The UC Libraries Digital Preservation Repository: Launching in Spring 2005, the digital preservation repository will offer a set of services for the controlled, orderly deposit of digital objects and the delivery of those objects between authorized users and long-term storage. Grant funding for the digital preservation repository has been received from the Institute of Museum and Library Services. [HTML]
* Preserving and persistently managing ejournals. The UC libraries have invested heavily in licensed content, but do not directly control the content. Because of this, the digital preservation program is investigating methods to preserve and manage these materials.
* Preserving online government and political materials: Funded by grants from the Library of Congress's National Digital Information Infrastructure and Preservation Program (NDIIPP) and The Andrew W. Mellon Foundation, these projects focus on identifying, collecting, and preserving web-based government and political information. In the process, they provide an understanding of strategies for web archiving in general.
* Press release: CDL receives $2.4 million Library of Congress grant to preserve online government and political materials. [DOC]

* Final report for The Andrew W. Mellon Foundation: Evaluating solutions for the capture, curation, and preservation of web-based government information. [PDF]

Developed in collaboration with national and international efforts, the digital preservation infrastructure adheres to established standards and open-source practices.

Preservation partners include the UC campus libraries and digital library and preservation researchers around the world.

Education, Communication & Assessment

The California Digital Library has a variety of education, communication, and assessment activities that introduce the organization to others and help further the understanding of digital libraries. Through this program, the CDL collaborates with staff at each campus to foster successful use of digital collections and services and informs University of California and its partners about the wide range of digital library services and developments.

In addition, the CDL considers it critical to understand the information needs of the UC community and characteristics of the use of its digital collections and services. These assessment activities are fundamental to the CDL's own education and the informed pursuit of improving service.

The education, communication, and assessment program allows the CDL to:

* Foster independent and successful use of CDL collections, services, and tools: Activities include establishing usability tools for the selection and design of collections and services, and working with the Evaluation Liaisons, the Users Council, and other service staff on the campuses to develop outreach and instructional materials. User guides and help are included with all major collections and services.

* Develop an understanding of the needs of CDL patrons and their use of CDL resources: Projects include soliciting information from patrons, performing needs assessments for service design and enhancements, and coordinating the production of quantitative and qualitative use data.
* Articulate CDL directions, goals, and activities for a variety of audiences: Methods and venues include this web site and a variety of publications, press releases, and communiqués.

CDL Technologies

The CDL Technologies group is responsible for the technical design, implementation, and operations of the California Digital Library in support of the plans and policies formulated by the University Librarian.

CDL technologies provide enabling infrastructure for campus libraries and other information organizations by:

* Investing in technologies and applications that help campus libraries and others build cost effective, customized services that support the use of the University's scholarly, cultural, and learning resources.
* Continuously experimenting with innovative technologies in the provision of scholarly information and in the development of new forms of scholarly communication.
* Defining architecture guidelines and standards in cooperation with the University community.
* Implementing new systems within this framework.

Future Directions

Looking ahead, the CDL technologies group is working to develop the full range of infrastructures requisite to the ingest, preservation, and presentation of information to scholarly communities.

The CDL recognizes that new directions must be

explored to leverage ingenuity in systems design for the delivery of content to users, and that these system's capabilities must be accessible, uniform, and well-characterized. The future lies in the services the CDL provides, not merely in the content the CDL preserves.

Partners & Research

Collaboration is a core value for the California Digital Library. The CDL's continuing success in delivering and sustaining digital collections and services for the University of California's teaching and research depends on its collaboration with the UC campuses as well as state, national, and international partners.

The CDL provides leadership to the digital library community through founding memberships in key organizations that are working to define and analyze library challenges and technological innovations. CDL staff members are active within many key standards development groups and initiatives.

In addition, the CDL has a very successful record of acquiring grants to explore strategic innovations in digital libraries. Granters have included the Andrew W. Mellon Foundation, the Library Services and Technology Act administered by the California State Library, the Institute of Museum and Library Services, and the Library of Congress.

Partners

The Library partners with the University of California's campus libraries and systemwide library planning to build and maintain a shared digital collection and a digital services infrastructure. In addition, the CDL partners with many other organizations based at UC, including museums, the UC Press, and the San Diego Supercomputer Center in order to expand the scope of its research and programs.

Outside of the UC, the CDL is deeply networked with national and international research, cultural, and education establishments. Through active memberships in several organizations, the CDL contributes to the development of digital libraries. Staff members participate in the definition of technical standards that support digital library activities, collections, and services.

Memberships and Standards Work

The CDL is a member of:

* Coalition for Networked Information
* Consortium for the Computer Interchange of Museum Information
* Council on Library and Information Resources (CLIR)
* COUNTER
* Digital Library Federation (DLF)
* EDUCAUSE
* International Coalition of Library Consortia (ICOLC)
* National Information Standards Organization (NISO)
* RLG
* Scholarly Publishing Academic Resources Coalition (SPARC)

CDL staff contribute to standards development efforts, including:

* Metadata Encoding and Transmission Standard (METS): CDL staff (Brian Tingle) serving on the editorial board.
* Open Archives Initiative (OAI): CDL staff serving on the steering committee.
* OpenURL: CDL staff serving on the National Information Standards Organization (NISO) Development Committee.
* Preservation Metadata: Implementation Strategies (PREMIS): CDL staff serving on this working group sponsored by the Online Computer Library Center (OCLC) and the Research Libraries Group (RLG).

* Shibboleth: CDL and UC staff serving on the Internet 2 development and implementation groups.
* Z39.50: CDL staff serving on the Implementers Group Advisory Board.

Research

With its partners, the California Digital Library is actively engaged in applied research that contributes to the development of digital library content and services and the progress of scholarly communication.

At the CDL, applied research takes several forms. Results have directly shaped digital library collections and services at the University of California and throughout California, and have had national and international impacts.

Grant-funded initiatives: Impacts of externally funded projects include refined digitization and encoding standards for cultural materials, best practices for creating and sustaining digital collections, deeper understanding of digital preservation methods and collaboration, expanded alternatives for scholarly publishing, and insights on user behavior toward print and digital materials. Grants totaling more than $1 million per year have been awarded from the Andrew W. Mellon Foundation, the Library Services and Technology Act administered by the California State Library, the Institute of Museum and Library Services, and the Library of Congress, among others.

Co-development: The CDL is in a unique position to help surface the interests and skills of stakeholder organizations, and support applied research and co-developments among them. For example, support from the CDL has helped California museums and libraries to develop their digital collections, the University's herbaria to collaborate in the creation of online collections and services, and the Electronic Cultural Atlas Initiative to build new tools.

Standards development: The CDL lends its staff to the principle community efforts to understand digital library technology and infrastructure requirements, and to define, test, and establish related standards. Staff have participated in standards work for content encoding, digitization, systems interoperability, and security and authentication. See a list of CDL memberships and standards work at the partners page.

Selective list of grant-funded activities:

* Preservation of web-based government information: Investigating of the technical alternatives for harvesting, organizing, and preserving web-based government information. $150,000 grant from the Andrew W. Mellon Foundation.
* Management of mixed print and digital collections: Systemwide Library Planning is exploring how scholars and libraries can best integrate and preserve collections of scholarly journals that are published in both print and digital forms. $670,000 grant from the Andrew W. Mellon Foundation.
* Preservation of UC library materials: Creating a pilot digital preservation repository for multi-institutional use, based on the Open Archive Information System (OAIS) model for digital preservation. $374,736 grant from the Institute of Museum and Library Services.
* Contributions to the National Digital Library collection: Supporting cooperation between the Online Archive of California (OAC) and the Library of Congress's National Digital Library Program. $600,000 grant from the Library of Congress.
* Best practices for digitizing cultural heritage materials and finding aids: Supporting the creation of and permanent access to standardized metadata and digital images through the OAC. $488,148 awarded in three grants from the California State Library's Library Services Technology Act (LSTA).
* Alternative forms of scholarly communication: Supporting experimentation in the dissemination of

research findings. $167,836 grant from the Scholarly Publishing Academic Resources Coalition (SPARC).

* Extension of library standards to museums: Evaluating the capabilities of Encoded Archival Descriptions, a digital finding aid technology, to integrate museum collection descriptions into the OAC collections. $828,533 awarded in two National Leadership grants from the Institute of Museum and Library Services.
* Establishment of the Japanese American Relocation Digital Archive (JARDA): Mining California's rich collections of Japanese American relocation materials to create JARDA. $358,724 grant from the Library Services and Technology Act, administered by the California State Library.

National Science Foundation's Digital Library Initiative–Phase 2: The CDL is working with UC Berkeley, UC Santa Barbara, Stanford, and the San Diego Supercomputer Center on the "InterLib" suite of California projects in the NSF-funded Digital Library Initiative.

9
Harvard University Digital Library

The Harvard University Library (HUL) is a department of the Central Administration that serves as the coordinating body for the more than 90 libraries that comprise the Harvard library system. HUL develops and implements library services and programs that are best provided centrally. These include the Office for Information Systems (which manages HOLLIS), the Harvard Depository (for off-site storage), the Weissman Preservation Center, the University Archives (including the Records Management Program), the Library Digital Initiative, and the Open Collections Program.

Harvard University launched the Library Digital Initiative (LDI) in July 1998 as a five-year program to develop the University's capacity to manage digital information by:

* creating the technical infrastructure to support the acquisition, organization, delivery, and archiving of digital library materials;
* providing a team of specialists to advise librarians and others in the University community on key issues in the digital environment;
* providing librarians and staff with experience in a wide range of technologies and digital materials; and,
* enriching the Harvard University Library collections with a significant set of digital resources

The Harvard Depository Mission

The Harvard Depository is a climate-controlled media storage and retrieval facility, owned and operated by Harvard

University, under the directorship of the Harvard University Library administration.

These guidelines and specifications were developed for the special conditions existing at the Harvard Depository and do not constitute recommendations to other entities. This document should not be utilized at other facilities without appropriate internal review.

The mission of the Harvard Depository is to promote effective use of space on the Harvard campus and the retention of financially and historically valuable resources by providing a secure, reliable, and cost-effective archival environment for the storage and retrieval of media.

Goals

There are five overarching goals that support the Harvard Depository's mission:

* protect and preserve the collections entrusted to our care;
* meet or exceed client and archival storage industry standards for services;
* expend funds prudently to the maximum benefit of clients and the University;
* conduct ongoing qualitative and quantitative measurement and continual analysis and reporting of performance; and
* sustain a work environment that promotes teamwork, cooperation, and communication as values supporting our mission.

Proposal for the Library

Introduction

Digital information is transforming the conduct of teaching and research. There are debates about the speed of change and the nature of the change, but there is no doubt that the creation, transmission, accessing, and archiving of information will increasingly be digital. The Harvard Library is already moving into the world of digital information.

Harvard must and will develop a digital library capacity. There are a number of reasons why such a development is required:

Necessity

Libraries, of necessity, reflect the world of scholarship and information. They acquire, disseminate, and preserve information in whatever form it is created by scholars and publishers; they provide teachers and researchers with materials in the forms those users desire. More and more of that material is being produced in digital form; more and more of users want access to such materials. Harvard has no choice but to develop the capacity to collect digital resources as it always has paper-based materials.

Functionality

Digital information can be used in ways that paper cannot: it need not be tied to a particular location; it can be transmitted more easily to users; it can be consulted by many users at once; it encompasses many media from text to quantitative data to visual and audio materials, allowing these to be combined; it can be searched, copied, and manipulated in ways unknown to print. A full explication of ways in which digital information is changing and enhancing scholarship and learning would require a much longer paper, but the evidence is overwhelming. Numerous classes at Harvard-undergraduate, graduate, and professional-use digital information in the teaching process. In many cases, this is a more efficient way for teachers to provide information and students to obtain it through electronic reserves, on-line texts, and on-line visual collections. In many cases digital information represents more: the availability of digital information is transforming the teaching and learning process by allowing students to explore widely across information sources, to combine materials in new ways, and to be more active and creative participants in the learning process.

Excellence

Effective movement into digital information is needed to maintain Harvard's special position of excellence. The Harvard University Library is the greatest academic library in the world. If any metric sets Harvard apart from other universities it is the Library. Furthermore, it is not only that the library per se is a major resource for teaching and research; the library is directly related to the quality of the other major university resource: its faculty. The library is a major factor is attracting and keeping faculty. If the library declines in quality so does the University.

Every year, the Association of Research Libraries ranks its member libraries on a standard indicator of library scale. Every year, the data array looks the same: there is a smooth progression upward across the 100-plus academic libraries with a major discontinuity-Harvard-alone at the top level. The ranking is largely based on the size of collections and the scale of operations. No one can catch Harvard in that ranking. However, if one were to add criteria for performance in the digital world, it would likely rank one third of the way down-below a number of the major universities with which it competes. As time goes on, the faculty and students will more and more want performance in the digital library world commensurate with what they have come to expect from the paper-based collections. If Harvard is to maintain its quality-not merely for competitive purposes but because it values the highest levels of teaching and research-it will have to increase the efforts and change the way of doing things.

The proposal outlines the changes in library operation and structure caused by the digital revolution, and recommends a strategy for responding to these changes. It describes a project to develop the institutional capacity to acquire, deliver, and archive digital information and it argues for a more coordinated approach to these tasks than is the Harvard norm. Harvard has no choice but to move decisively into the world of digital information. The research and teaching obligations and the changing nature of the information needed to support those obligations require action and investment.

A Coordinated Approach

Given that many libraries must collect, deliver, and archive digital information to it needs a centralized University-wide project and not rely on distributed local activity, the norm for library operations at Harvard? A central, coordinated project is needed for at least three reasons:

Digital information is different. When a book is acquired, it resides in a single library. When a digital resource is put on the network, it can be equally available to all. Further, traditional materials are sold in small units with a relatively low unit price, and purchasing decisions are virtually always local. Digital materials are being marketed in larger and much more costly units, and both decisions to purchase and the related cost-sharing negotiations frequently involve many separate Harvard units.

Shared services are more efficient. The development of digital libraries involves a wide range of highly specialized technical skills, and duplicating those skills in each library would be both difficult and wasteful. Likewise digital libraries require a set of common infrastructure services, that need not be replicated in each individual library. Some hardware components exhibit significant economies of scale, including storage systems, one of the chief cost components of digital library systems. Software to support commonly used services can be licensed once for the entire University.

Integration improves service. For the library user, having a unified and coherent way to find what is available, a single means of accessing secured resources, the fewest interfaces to digital materials, and the smallest set of required desktop applications represents significantly better service than if each library were to implement varied ways of doing similar things.

Harvard's libraries and library users have benefited for many years from the integrated, shared services of HOLLIS. The digital library will likewise benefit from coordinated development and common services. The absence of a coordinated infrastructure will inevitably generate duplicative and incompatible efforts in individual libraries, duplication that will (in the absence of a University-wide effort) happen soon in our current environment of exploding digital resources.

Proposal Overview

The Harvard's digital library like other counterparts will be built over many decades as the world of digital information evolves. Rather it is proposed to launch Harvard's digital library effort, to give it the initial momentum, momentum that it is expected to be carried through regular library operations once digital libraries mature and digital formats become a norm. We are in a period of discontinuity, one where none of the old forms have been replaced, but new ones surround us, demanding attention. It is therefore proposed a one-time effort to provide special resources to help cope with these extraordinary times.

The proposed project will:

* create the first-generation technical infrastructure to support storage of and access to digital library materials;
* make available a staff of specialists to advise librarians (and other University personnel working in related areas) about a number of key issues related to digital materials, including digital reformatting, metadata, licensing, and archiving;
* give librarians and technologists experience with a wide range of technologies and digital materials on which to base future decisions and development;
* provide library users with at least one significant set of

digital resources to support current teaching and research activities.

At the end of the five year period it is expected that Harvard will have the capacity to collect, organize, serve, and archive digital materials with the sophistication and ease with which it now manages traditional media, and that use of the digital collections will be part of the daily activity of students and scholars across the University. The acquisition, organization, and management of digital information should be on a firm footing as new information sources appear. The libraries will have a solid base for adaptation to the inevitable market and technical changes that will continue to take place in the digital world.

Digital Libraries Elsewhere

Harvard is, of course, not alone in facing the need for an extraordinary initiative related to digital libraries. Most of the peer institutions have concerted programs underway, in some cases programs of considerable magnitude. Among the most notable are those at:

* The ***Library of Congress***, which has begun developing the National Digital Library, with a target 5-year budget of $60 million (including a $3 million annual appropriation from Congress and significant private contributions). The program has already generated a considerable collection of primary source materials related to the development of the United States, a collection receiving heavy use from around the world.
* The ***University of California*** system, which has recently created The California Digital Library program to acquire and archive digital materials for all 9 University campuses. The project budget for the initial year is $3 million, which does not include much of the infrastructure costs supported elsewhere in the University's budget.

* The ***University of Michigan***, which in 1993 initiated its Digital Library Program with the intention of creating a "comprehensive (i.e., campuswide in perspective), coherent (i.e., logical in its organization and scope), and coordinated (i.e., supported by systems and standards to promote effective access)" digital library collection. The digital material now available at Michigan are impressive in their scope and variety. Michigan's digital infrastructure has enabled it to win a continuing series of grants for content and program development.
* The ***University ofVirginia***, which has created technical centers specializing in a wide range of digital information, including: Digital Image Center, Digital Media and Music Center, Electronic Text Center, Geographic Information Center, Social Sciences Data Center, and the Special Collections Digital Center. Together these represent a wide array of resources (a fact that faculty coming to Harvard from Virginia have pointed out to Harvard librarians).
* The ***UK Higher Education Funding Council***, which has mounted a 3-year, 15 million-pound, Electronic Libraries Programme to fund university-based digital library projects in a number of areas, including experimentation with electronic journals, digital preservation, and training.

The proposed program would not put Harvard at the "cutting edge" of digital library developments. Rather it is proposed to profit from the pioneering efforts of others who have invested in research and exploration of the many difficult issues in digital libraries. The program is intended to build on current knowledge to create a practical, large-scale infrastructure that will be of daily use in building our electronic collections as the world of publishing moves into the digital age.

Project Activities

Developing Infrastructure

Infrastructure is the collection of common systems and services that make it possible to store, organize, and access digital materials. Among the key elements to be addressed in the project are:

* **Catalogs and indexes.** The hallmark of a library is organization, a structure that helps users identify and locate what is available. The HOLLIS catalog will be a key component of our infrastructure, but it is not adequate for many types of materials likely to be in the digital collections, including:
    * photographs, prints, and other visual materials
    * contents of archival collections
    * journal articles.

Building these separate catalogs and linking them in a coherent structure is critical to making the digital collections useful. It is a technical and intellectual task of considerable magnitude, and one made all the more pressing by the scale and breadth of Harvard's collections.

* **Controlling access.** Much of the digital collection will likely be owned by others, and Harvard will only have a license permitting use. Other materials may be the property of Harvard, but we will want to control access for legal, contractual, or economic reasons. Securing access to digital materials can be thought of as a two-dimensional matrix composed of:
    * the user (how do we know for certain who this user is? what category is this user in?)
    * the digital item (which user classes can access this item? what use rights do they have to use this item: view a description? view a low-grade version? view a high-definition version? print a copy?).

* **Storage.** Large digital collections involve many issues:
    * cost effective large-scale storage of hardware and software, including the capability to store digital items on a variety of devices with varying cost and performance characteristics
    * systematic back-up* disaster recovery plans and facilities
    * media migration to protect against data loss
    * coherence between stored objects and the data about those objects ("metadata") that makes them useable.

Scale changes storage requirements. Storing hundreds of thousands of digital objects and information about them requires tools, discipline, and systematic operations. A digital repository resembles in many ways the Harvard Depository-its nature is determined more by the scale of operation than by the specific nature of the materials stored. To work well, both require careful professional management.

* **Interface.** The user interface for printed materials is inherent in the carrier (a book, a journal, a newspaper-each embodies its own interface). Digital materials are frequently separate from the interface, and the same object can be delivered through many different interfaces. One of the difficulties in the current environment is that there is a dramatic proliferation of interfaces, a proliferation that is causing user confusion and frustration. While one cannot hope to do away with the need to use many different system interfaces, a shared set of frequently used interfaces for such common actions as the following will noticeably simplify the use of the digital library:
    * searching bibliographic databases
    * viewing images of digitized journal articles or other page-based materials

* navigating through descriptions of archival collections.

Acquiring Digital Resources

The content of Harvard's digital collection will come from many sources, and will be distributed across many systems, within Harvard and without. Sources will include authors, commercial and non-profit publishers, government agencies, value-added aggregators, other universities and libraries, and scholarly societies. It is anticipated that the landscape of players and products will evolve in complex and unexpected ways over the next decade. In this project they will both assist with the general acquisition and creation of content by Harvard libraries and begin creating a significant collection of content in specific areas.

The first two project activities relate to materials created outside of Harvard:

1. **Assistance with digital acquisitions.** The libraries are buying an increasing number of databases, digital reference works, and electronic journals. The acquisition process is increasingly complex, involving such questions as:
   * are there (or will there soon be) alternate sources for the same or equivalent materials?
   * will the delivery system fit Harvard's security and access systems?
   * is this the right interface for this material?
   * are there appropriate provisions for long-term, archival access?
   * is there adequate provision for "fair use"?
   * what parts of Harvard should share in the cost of providing this resource?
   * can this resource be effectively used over the Internet, or is a local copy needed?

- are there adequate service guarantees in the contract?
- does the contract protect Harvard against liability claims?
- is the authorized user base defined appropriately for Harvard?

These issues are new to most librarians and addressing them requires specialized knowledge and understanding of both the technical and the legal environment.

2. **Integration of outside resources.** Much of the content of Harvard's digital collection will be held on systems outside the University. Because there are few standards or conventions for how such systems should operate, these systems tend to be designed in an astonishing variety of ways. Thus a significant effort is needed to integrate them into Harvard's local environment, in such areas as:
   - securing access
   - integrating with local interfaces
   - linking content and indexes
   - relating electronic content with Harvard's holdings of paper equivalents or of related materials
   - integrating searches across multiple related databases.

One of the key advantages of digital resources is that they can be functionally brought together for the user regardless of their physical location or technical format. Such integration however requires effort, both technical and intellectual, and the resulting smooth operation and navigation is one of the key contributions of libraries to the digital arena.

In addition to acquiring digital materials from elsewhere, there is an ever-increasing amount of interest at Harvard (not just within the libraries, but also in other areas including the museums, research projects, and classroom support) converting materials from traditional to digital format. Motivation for digital conversion includes the preservation of content when the original format is endangered, providing enhanced functionality, and improving access. This program will provide assistance in addressing many of the issues raised by these conversion projects.

Four additional project activities relate to materials converted locally:

3. **Conversion formats and methodologies.** Even something as seemingly straightforward as digital imaging, which is essentially the simple recording of a picture digitally, involves many issues. There are numerous recording formats, varying in the amount of detail captured, likely functional longevity (conventions and standards in this area evolve rapidly), the software that is required to capture, display, or print the image, the size of the resulting digital object, and the ability to render color. For the conversion of text, there are issues of markup (tagging added to text to identify and label its parts), for which varying standards and conventions are available, standards that affect usability, archivability, and the software needed for manipulation and display. For any digital format there are generally many conversion technologies available, again involving tradeoffs among functionality, cost, effort required, likely longevity, and compatibility with various technical environments. All of these issues involve technical knowledge and experience. The availability of appropriate technical assistance as the project is designed will significantly affect the utility of the product, the cost of the conversion, and the longevity of the result.

4. **Metadata.** To be useable by people or software, digital materials need to be described systematically:
   * For the user, this description is usually a catalog

entry, providing index terms as well as a description of the item and location information. There are many differing practices in use today, both local ones and those adopted by various communities (current examples include standards adopted by research libraries, arts and cultural heritage museums, visual arts libraries, botanical or biological systematics collections, archives, and manuscripts libraries).

* For the curator responsible for a digital object, there are many pieces of administrative information needed: information about the date and technique used for object conversion (of significance for media refreshing or format conversion), whether a copy is considered archival (which will affect how it is stored and formatted), and what access restrictions apply. Standards or conventions for which administrative information should be recorded, and how it should be encoded, are not yet common.

* For software, the technical format of a digital object must be recorded (affecting what software is needed to render or use the object), how a given object relates to other digital objects (affecting how the interface provides navigation through a related set of materials such as images of the pages of a journal article), and the mark-up standard followed (describing the meaning of the tagging to be found in a text). There are an enormous number of examples and conventions for such "structural" metadata in use today, some standardized (e. g., the various "document type definitions" for text marked up in Standard Generalized Markup Language), many local or proprietary (such as the page-relationship data used in commercial electronic document management systems).

Again, this is an area where technical expertise and experience are required for intelligent decisions to be made in designing projects.

5. **Conversion process design.** Most conversion projects involve the expenditure of significant resources. A well designed workflow, the choice of the right technologies and service providers, and appropriate quality control standards and procedures are critical to controlling costs and conversion time, and improving the resulting product. This is an area where technical expertise and experience will make a significant difference in project design, affecting cost, usability, and longevity.
6. **Ownership marking.** When Harvard owns the rights to a digital object, there may be concerns about controlling legitimate reuse of that object. The University may want to allow general scholarly access to its resources, but to control (and perhaps profit from) their reuse in commercial publications. "Electronic watermarking" and similar technologies can provide ways of tracking the origin of an object and provide assistance in controlling the use and flow of owned resources. Such techniques are becoming available in the marketplace, but choosing the right strategy will require careful investigation and analysis.

Project Structure

A 5-year project is proposed to be based in the University Library. The project would be managed under the direction of a governance committee of representatives from faculties and libraries. The committee would be responsible for setting priorities for project activities, for monitoring progress and costs, and for allocating the incentive fund (discussed below). In particular, it is recommended that in addition to the normal month-to-month monitoring of the project, the governance committee conduct a formal review in the third year, to ensure that the project continues to be useful and its directions appropriate. The rapid evolution of the digital environment requires vigilance. Much will change over the course of the project.

The University Library would create a project team of systems developers and technical consultants, who would be responsible for the creation of the technical infrastructure and for providing assistance and consulting advice to library staff and others at Harvard developing or delivering digital resources. The University Library would also procure adequate hardware and software for operating the infrastructure and housing digital materials when needed.

Digital library developments must be driven by collection content and by relevance to the University's academic mission, not by technology. The work on infrastructure and integration discussed above cannot be done in the abstract, divorced from actual digital library materials.

Therefore a critical part of this project is the development of a digital collection that provides both ongoing utility to Harvard users, and experience on which to base sound design and development decisions. At Harvard, building library collections is a decentralized responsibility, with decisions about what to collect made at a level close to the researchers and students. A program to develop content therefore cannot be executed centrally. Instead, it is proposed for creation of a funding pool to be used to encourage the rapid development of a critical mass of digital materials, in order to:

* provide real-world experience with the use of digital library resources
* provide a set of materials on which to base infrastructure development
* test and demonstrate the utility of Harvard's digital library developments.

This incentive fund would be used to help support digital item creation or acquisition by the individual libraries, based on the following criteria:

* the materials would have to contribute meaningfully to building a critical mass of resources in a limited number of topical areas (they suggest using social science materials related to contemporary social issues or policy development, or materials related to one of the interfaculty initiatives, as these would be useful in all of the Harvard Faculties);
* projects would need to utilize or, even better, contribute to the development of the common infrastructure;
* materials should represent a variety of types of digital resources, so as to build experience at Harvard with a wide range of digital materials and to provide information on the relative utility of various resource types.

Most projects receiving support from the incentive fund are expected to involve significant matching effort or resources from the individual library (or libraries) involved.

Costs

There are three categories of costs to be considered for the digital library developments proposed here.

* First, there are the direct project costs for staff, hardware, software, HOLLIS II, and space and overhead. These are estimated to cost $7 million. In addition it is proposed to have an Incentive fund of $5 million, for a total project cost of $12 million.
* Second, for digital libraries to succeed, the University will need to provide a number of other types of infrastructure applicable not only to digital libraries but also to other network and computing applications at Harvard. Examples of such infrastructure include network capacity, user authentication facilities, distributed printing facilities, support for local networks and workstations, and electronic classroom facilities and support. These are not directly attributable to the digital library but are a necessary condition for it to succeed.

* Third, the discontinuity of the digital revolution is causing severe strain on library collection budgets. The explosion of electronic resources on the market represents an increase in the pool of materials appropriate for the libraries to collect. Further, today little of the new material displaces traditional resources. For the next several years at least, the libraries will therefore be faced with demands both to continue collecting as they have in the past and to acquire the new electronic formats. Since the proposed incentive fund is intended to be limited in both time and subject scope, libraries will be faced with the need to find significant new revenue to continue collecting as they have in the past, or they must reduce the scope of their collecting.

Conclusion

The world of information-and the lives of those whose work depends on it-is being transformed. Key decisions affecting the ways in which online resources can be used, the standards, and the new solutions, are being shaped by the active participants. Work relating to digital libraries has been underway for over a decade. To date, Harvard has moved cautiously in digital libraries. The dramatic increase in the rate of development of electronic information in the past two years makes it inappropriate that they continue in this cautious manner. The explosion in the publishing and use of digital information requires to act now.

The development of a digital library for Harvard is not a threat to the remarkable history of its existing libraries. It is instead a powerful complement to those collections. If Harvard intends to be among the leading players in defining new directions for its outstanding academic programs, in shaping information policies for the digital world, and in creating the educational environment for the new millennium, it will need the best possible access to a full array of information resources, both print and digital. The development of a digital library, with the concomitant commitments to building a sound technological infrastructure and developing a community of highly skilled library and computing professionals, is a necessary step for the University.

For the libraries at Harvard, the years ahead will pose significant challenges to provide the best possible balance between print-based collections and digital resources. At present, the lack of a defined infrastructure for a digital library and the fragmented nature of digital content make it very difficult for the libraries to respond to the needs of the teaching and research programs of the University. The program we outline will allow the Harvard libraries to be effective providers of information to the users in the most cost-efficient way possible. Commitment to the coordinated development of a digital library program for Harvard will provide each of the libraries the opportunity to focus its attention on acquiring access to needed content, rather than crafting idiosyncratic solutions to maintain digital library developments. The libraries at Harvard are poised to carry out a vital role in assuring integrated access to both traditional and digital information resources. To do so effectively, there needs to be an institutional commitment to and a corollary investment in development of an operational infrastructure for a digital library.

10
Digital Library of Georgia

The Digital Library of Georgia is a GALILEO initiative based at the University of Georgia Libraries that works together with Georgia's libraries, archives, museums, and other institutions of cultural heritage to provide access to the cultural and historical resources of the state of Georgia. This primary mission is accomplished through the ongoing development, maintenance, and preservation of digital collections and online digital library resources.

The Digital Library of Georgia also provides digital library, photographic, and micrographic services, and supports the instruction, research, and service missions of GALILEO and the University System of Georgia through collaboration with university faculty, students, and staff, and through participation on local and national levels in the development of digital library standards, practice, and technology. The Digital Library facilitates cooperative ventures with other organizations and provides leadership for cooperative digital initiatives throughout the state.

The Library works together with Georgia's libraries, archives, museums, and other institutions of cultural heritage to provide access to the cultural and historical resources of the state of Georgia. This primary mission is accomplished through the ongoing development, maintenance, and preservation of digital collections and online digital library resources. These may include materials such as original manuscripts, typescripts, books, photographs, maps, sheet music, posters and broadsides, newspapers, primary source materials on microfilm, audio, video, and other formats.

The DLG participates on local and national levels in the

development of digital library standards, practice, and technology, facilitates cooperative ventures with other organizations, and provides leadership for cooperative digital initiatives throughout the state.

The Digital Library of Georgia is also a department of the University of Georgia Libraries that provides digital library, photographic, and micrographic services, and supports the instruction, research, and service missions of GALILEO and the University System of Georgia through collaboration with university faculty, students, and staff.

The Library has four functional units:

Digital Library of Georgia Production Center

The Digital Library of Georgia Production Center supports the mission and goals of the Digital Library of Georgia by developing, maintaining, and preserving collections of digital content in collaboration with University of Georgia Libraries' and GALILEO staff.

Digital Library of Georgia Teaching and Learning Center

The Digital Library of Georgia Teaching and Learning Center supports the mission of the Digital Library of Georgia by providing support for instruction and learning for University students, faculty, and staff. The Center provides a physical space and technology for instruction and works closely with University and Library faculty in the development of instructional materials and programs. These activities directly support the Digital Library of Georgia's mission to provide access to cultural and historical resources of the state of Georgia.

Photographic Services

Photographic Services supports the mission of the Digital Library of Georgia and the University Libraries by working closely with the Digital Library of Georgia Production Center to provide digital imaging services for Digital Library of Georgia projects. Photographic Services also provides quality photographic and digital imaging services to patrons of the University of Georgia Libraries special collections libraries and University students, faculty, and staff.

Micrographic Services/Georgia Newspaper Project

Micrographic Services supports the mission of the Digital Library of Georgia and the University Libraries by preserving collections of materials related to the history and culture of Georgia for ongoing access and providing micrographic reproduction services to Library patrons and University students, faculty, and staff. Micrographic Services has primary responsibility for the Georgia Newspaper Project, part of the United States Newspaper Program.

Guiding Principles

* *Usability and accessibility.* Build highly usable and accessible collections to make resources available to as wide a range of researchers, scholars, students, and the general public as possible.
* *Standards and best practices.* Make use of standards, best practices, and open systems whenever possible to ensure longevity of and ongoing access to digital, photographic, and micrographic resources. Contribute to development of these standards and best practices by participation and collaboration with other digital library projects.
* *Added value.* Provide not only digital facsimiles of historical and cultural materials, but strive to include rich background, contextual information, description, and metadata to promote deeper analysis and greater understanding of the collections and materials. Likewise, develop and implement digital library tools and services to promote enhanced interpretation, context, and understanding.
* *Copyright.* Respect the rights of copyright owners by observing current laws and regulations regarding

copyright and fair use. Monitor and observe developing legislation and support active involvement.

* *Digital preservation.* Maintain and promote awareness and understanding of preservation of digital collections and take steps throughout the life cycle of digital materials to ensure ongoing access and usability.
* *Appropriate use of technology.* Implementation of new technology will follow the mission and goals of the Digital Library, rather than technology for its own sake. The Digital Library will maintain awareness of digital library and technclogical developments.

Goals of the Library

Build a sustainable and scalable digital library infrastructure.

Build comprehensive digital collections that reflect the full wealth of Georgia's history and culture and ensure fair representation of traditionally under-represented groups.

Preserve library collections, including sensitive cultural and historical resources through appropriate means such as photographic and micrographic reproduction.

Facilitate and cooperate in cooperative ventures with other organizations to build digital collections, resources, and services.

Contribute to the development of standards and best practices by participation at multiple levels including local, national, and international.

Provide high quality photographic and digital imaging services to University of Georgia library patrons and University students, faculty, and staff.

Promote instruction, teaching, and learning by providing instructional space and technology and working with university and library faculty to develop instructional resources and programs.

Collection Development

The Digital Library of Georgia, working together with Georgia's libraries, archives, museums, and other institutions of cultural heritage, provides access to the cultural and historical resources of the state of Georgia through ongoing development, maintenance, and preservation of online digital collections and resources. Original formats included may be text-based, including manuscripts, letters, diaries, and published works such as books and pamphlets, photographs, maps, art, artifacts, audio and video, graphic materials including architectural plans and drawings, and microfilm.

The Audience of the Digital Library of Georgia consists of five segments: Casual User, Student / K-12 / Lifelong Learner, Information Seeker / Hobbyist, Scholar / Researcher, Government / Business Community. (More information)

Collections, materials, or items may be nominated for digitization by any interested party using the Digital Library of Georgia Digitization Nomination Form.

Collections nominated for digitization and / or inclusion in the Digital Library of Georgia will be judged based on the following criteria.

Proposed materials or collections must conform to the mission of the Digital Library of Georgia and be related to the culture and history of the state of Georgia. Materials that are restricted by the donor or other owner will not be digitized unless permission can be obtained.

Materials that are clearly in the public domain will be given priority for digitization. Where public domain status is questionable, a decision will be made on a case by case basis. When materials are under copyright restrictions, they will not be digitized unless permission is likely to be easily obtainable.

Materials or collections that are completely or partially described, captioned, labeled, processed, or cataloged will be given priority for digitization. Other instances will be handled on a case by case basis depending on factors such as the type and depth of description required, need for research, etc.

Materials that are hard to access due to preservation concerns or are only available to a limited audience due to security restrictions will be given priority for digitization.

Materials that are heavily used by researchers, other patrons, or staff will be given greater priority for digitization.

Materials that represent the cultural, political, social, geographic, and/or economic diversity of the state of Georgia will be given priority.

Materials that have high research, artifactual, or evidential value and/or are of particular interest to a key audience will have high priority for digitization.

Materials for which access will be substantially improved by digitization and which have a high potential for added value in the digital environment will be given priority. Examples of added value that the materials may lend themselves to include:

Creation and/or addition of supplemental resources to allow users to better understand, navigate, and use the collection

Linkages between materials

Virtual collections of materials based around a creator, topic, subject, or similar theme

New metadata, description, and finding aids in electronic form

The ability to search through the creation of electronic text

New ways to use or analyze the originals

Duplication of Effort

Materials that are publicly available in digital form elsewhere at a level of quality that meets the needs of the audience of the Digital Library of Georgia will not be digitized. Note that the DLG Portal Service may link to items related to the mission of the Digital Library of Georgia.

Cooperative Potential

If the materials have the potential to be related to others held by different repositories or organizations, including materials already digitized or being considered for digitization, the priority for digitization is higher if it is likely that a cooperative or multi-collection digitization initiative may result.

Availability of Local or Additional Resources

Following on cooperative potential, if a repository or other organization can provide support in the form of staff time, equipment, or funding - especially at a local basis - to digitize materials to the standards required by the Digital Library of Georgia those collections may be given greater priority to take advantage of these opportunities.

Technology

Materials for which appropriate technology, processes, and best practices already exist for digitization will generally have priority. Projects that explore or require implementation of new technologies will be considered depending on the availability of resources and funding.

DLG Portal Service

The DLG Portal Service is a forthcoming project of the Digital Library of Georgia and is not currently active.

The DLG Portal Service links historical and cultural collections digitized by the DLG and held locally in GALILEO with digital collections, materials, sites, items or similar resources held by cultural and/or other non-profit organizations throughout the state and elsewhere by means of a selective portal service. The core of the portal service is a metadata catalog containing descriptive information about each resource.

The DLG Portal Service will record metadata about and link to sites meeting the following criteria:

* Provides digitized resources or finding aids for collections in Georgia's cultural institutions or resources representing Georgia's history and culture
* Makes the resource available at no cost
* Has a plan for ongoing sustainability and maintenance
* Respects copyright by ensuring that materials are in the public domain or cleared for public distribution
* Priority will be given to sites containing cultural materials digitized in accordance with standard best practices for digital imaging recommended by the Digital Library of Georgia

Ownership

The Digital Library of Georgia does not claim ownership of digital objects linked to from the DLG Portal Service. Ownership remains with the originating site. Note that collections digitized and mounted by the Digital Library of Georgia and GALILEO are linked to from the DLG Portal Service in the same way as other participating sites. Metadata created by the Digital Library of Georgia and included in the DLG Portal Service remains the property of the Digital Library of Georgia, but may be freely copied and shared as long as credit is given.

Accuracy

Responsibility for accuracy of data, facts, and information presented rests with the institution providing the digital resource. The Digital Library of Georgia does not warrant any information on the sites linked to by the portal. The Digital Library of Georgia recommends that all sites have a means of collection information regarding the content accuracy and a polity for site review and revision.

Accessibility

The DLG Portal Service strives to comply with accessibility standards developed as part of the Web Access Initiative of the World Wide Web Consortium available at http://www.w3.org/WAI/. However, the Digital Library of Georgia does not guarantee that sites linked to by the DLG Portal will comply with these accessibility standards.

Removal Policy

A site may be removed from the DLG Portal at the discretion of the Digital Library of Georgia for one or more of the following:

* Site is not consistently available and reliable
* Inaccurate data, facts, or information
* Proven violation of copyright
* Site or content is no longer available for free to the public

Copyright and Citation Information

The digital reproductions included in the Digital Library of Georgia have been made available for use in research, teaching (including distribution to classes), and private study. For these purposes one may reproduce (print, make photocopies, or download) materials from this web site without prior permission, on the condition of providing proper attribution of the source in all copies.

Because the materials in the Digital Library of Georgia come from a number of repositories within the state of Georgia, it uses the following form for citation:

[title of item when available], [name of collection], [name of repository], presented in the Digital Library of Georgia

Examples: Men Picking Cotton, Robert E. Williams Photographs, 1872-1898, Hargrett Rare Book and Manuscript Library, presented in the Digital Library of Georgia

Cornelius C. Platter Civil War Diary, 1864 - 1865, Hargrett Rare Book and Manuscript Library, presented in the Digital Library of Georgia

The materials and pages included in the Digital Library of Georgia may be linked to freely from other Web pages and Internet resources.

Frequently Asked Questions

Digitization of historical materials?

* More people can access and use unique, highly valuable, and often fragile materials
* Users can view the materials from any computer connected to the Internet, any time of day
* Searchable text allows users to conduct research in ways not possible before
* Users gain an understanding of the context of the materials in history through associated supplementary resources such as timelines and historical overviews
* Libraries can build "virtual collections" made up of related materials that are physically separated between repositories
* Digitized Materials can be used in new and exciting ways for research and instruction when combined with the communications facilities of the Internet

Digitization?

Selection of materials and collections to be included in the Digital Library of Georgia is guided by the Digital Library's Collection Development Policy.

Georgia HomePLACE

The Georgia Department of Archives and History (Office of Secretary of State), the Office of Public Library Services (Board of Regents, University System of Georgia), and the Digital Library of Georgia and GALILEO (University System of Georgia) are collaborating on the long-range project called Georgia HomePLACE (Providing Libraries and Archives Electronically) to digitize valuable Georgia family and local history records and make them available as part of the Digital Library of Georgia and GALILEO. During the first phase of the project, the following resources will be made available: *Vanishing Georgia* Historic Photograph Collection; Georgia

County Marriage Records; Georgia Confederate Veterans Pension Application Files; Georgia Historical Map Collections; and other unique Georgia archival resources. The materials for Georgia HomePLACE will be coordinated locally by Georgia Public Library Systems under the Office of Public Library Services. The Digital Library of Georgia, while including the Georgia HomePLACE project, will also include collections and resources from Georgia's colleges and universities (especially the University System of Georgia), and other historical societies, museums, and cultural heritage repositories.

More information about the Georgia HomePLACE project may be found at the project's Web site:

http://www.public.lib.ga.us/homeplace/

Funding

As a GALILEO initiative based at the University of Georgia Libraries, most of the funding for the Digital Library of Georgia comes from GALILEO, the University of Georgia, and other state sources. Grants from institutions such as the Andrew W. Mellon Foundation, the Institute for Library and Museum Services (IMLS), the Georgia Historical Records Advisory Board (GHRAB), the Taylor Foundation, and other sources also support current and past Digital Library Projects.

By nominating materials to be included in the Digital Library of Georgia, libraries, archives, museums, and other historical repositories throughout the state can help in the effort to obtain ongoing funding for the Digital Library.

New projects and collections

The Projects & Collections list provides information on newly available projects, ongoing resources, and forthcoming online collections being created by current DLG projects.

Historical materials

The Digital Library of Georgia is currently building a list of historical materials and collections related to the history and culture of Georgia from libraries, archives, museums, and other institutions of cultural heritage around the state. Selected collections may be digitized and made available online in the Digital Library of Georgia and GALILEO.

Historical materials

The DLG is planning the introduction of a Portal to Georgia History in the future to pull together high quality web sites relevant to Georgia's history and culture. More information on how sites will be selected may be found in the Digital Library's Collection Development Policy.

Use of Library materials

The digital reproductions included in the Digital Library of Georgia have been made available for use in research, teaching (including distribution to classes), and private study. For these purposes one may reproduce (print, make photocopies, or download) materials from this web site without prior permission, on the condition to provide proper attribution of the source in all copies.

Those interested in publishing or other commercial uses of materials should contact the repository responsible for the custody of the original materials. Web pages for DLG collections include a link to the holding repository where the contact information may be found. Note that some DLG collections contain related materials from multiple repositories.

Reproductions of materials

Because the items included in the digital library of Georgia come from a variety of repositories throughout the state, reproductions such as photographs, negatives, or photocopies of materials should be obtained directly from the holding repository. Availability of these services depends on the individual repository holding the original materials. Web pages for DLG collections include a link to the holding repository where the contact information may be found. Note that some DLG collections contain related materials from multiple repositories.

Linking a site

Anyone may link to the Digital Library of Georgia online collections without permission from the Digital Library of Georgia.

11
Indiana University Digital Library

The Indiana University Digital Library Program (DLP) is dedicated to the production and maintenance of a wide range of high-quality networked resources for scholars and students at Indiana University and elsewhere. The Digital Library Program is a collaborative effort of the Indiana University Libraries, the Office of the Vice President for Information Technology, and the university research faculty with leadership from the School of Library and Information Science. This collaboration will capitalize on the institutional capabilities of this university, focusing university resources on digital library projects that support the teaching and research of IU faculty, support the learning and research of IU students, and foster research about the digital library.

The overarching benefit for the students, faculty, and staff of Indiana University will be access to an ever-widening range of digital library resources and services, including full-text online databases, faculty research, classroom materials, multimedia digital resources, electronic journals, and digital libraries from all over the world.

GOALS

- To increase the number and range of digital resources available for faculty and students;
- To offer digital library services and supporting technologies that are sustainable, scaleable, compatible with the university's technology infrastructure, and interoperable with national and international digital library initiatives;

- To promote and support the scholarly use of digital content and networked information resources by students and faculty at IU;
- To discover and promote currently available digital technologies that can revitalize teaching and enhance learning;
- To address key research questions from user-centered, collections-centered, and system-centered perspectives, their inter-relatedness and the importance of their balance;
- To conduct a program of research to advance the state of knowledge and practice in digital libraries, and the social, organizational, technological, and human factors involving the uses and users of digital libraries;
- To establish a national and international reputation for developing a premier digital library at Indiana University;
- To collaborate with colleagues at other colleges, universities, and research libraries, nationally and internationally in the development of an inter-institutional and international federation of distributed digital libraries.

PARTICIPANTS

The Digital Library Program encompasses all campuses of Indiana University. The program is directed through the steering committee comprised of three partners, the Libraries, University Information Technology Services (UITS), and the School of Library and Information Science (SLIS). The current Administrative Team includes librarians, staff and information technologists from the Bloomington and Indianapolis Libraries and UITS.

PROGRAM AREAS

The IU Digital Library Program (IUDLP) will continue focus on a limited number of high priority program areas that include already successful digital library initiatives, development of new digital library services, research and development into digital library technologies, and various collaborations and partnerships.

The criteria for selecting digital library activities for support include:

* Existing digital services that have demonstrated their usefulness to students or faculty.
* Current projects to which it has committed resources.
* New projects that offer widespread benefits to students or faculty.
* New projects that contribute to teaching and learning, and offer research opportunities to faculty.
* New projects that contribute to teaching and learning, and offer technology development opportunities for librarians or technologists.

The activities meet one or more of these criteria. To expand list the Digital Library Program Team solicits other project ideas and offers interested individuals help in planning and obtaining funding for other projects that fall within the scope of digital library initiatives.

Ongoing Digital Library Services

School of Music Digital Audio Library.

The Variations Project will expand its collection of digitized audio to meet instructional and research needs. In addition, the project will begin to provide access to image-based content, including CD booklets, liner notes, and musical scores. Changes to the current audio client and server will be made to migrate audio delivery to current protocols for multimedia delivery and resource reservation over IP. Access to Variations will be expanded from delivery in the Music Library, to other locations within the campus and university as network and intellectual property issues permit, including student computing labs, other libraries, faculty offices, and student housing. Experiments in providing inter-institutional access to music collections will be pursued in cooperation with other universities. URL: http://www.dlib.indiana.edu/variations/.

Electronic text Resources for the Humanities.

LETRS will expand its SGML encoded electronic collections available over the WWW. In addition to providing access to commercially published collections, LETRS will expand its electronic texts by participating in and supporting new projects, using as a model the ongoing Victorian Women Writers Project. LETRS will also investigate collaborating with the Preservation Department, which is creating and storing digital page images for preservation, in the conversion of page images to full-text searchable collections. LETRS will also explore collaboration opportunities with Indiana University faculty scholars and the IU Press. Further, IUL and UITS will review and redefine the mission of LETRS with respect to its provision of public services and its role in developing and managing a specialized digital (CD-ROM) collection of works in the humanities, including English, Classics, Religious Studies, Philosophy, History, Languages, Linguistics and more. URL: http://www.indiana.edu/~letrs/.

DIDO (Digital Images Online).

The Digital Library Program supports a collection of low-resolution (72 dpi) digital images selected from the Slide Library collection of over 300,000 images. The image database, created in 1996, represents all historical periods and all media. As of August 2001, the database contains over 17,000 images, which are used to support upwards of 10 class-oriented web pages in the Art History Department each semester. Beginning fall semester 2001 it is expanding access to anyone an Indiana University campus for other educational purposes, via keyword searching and browsing. It is appointing an advisory group that will meet through the coming academic year to advise on enhancements to DIDO and ways to provide improved service to users outside the Department of Art History, on all campuses. Currently, image selection for DIDO is determined by the teaching needs of the School of Fine Arts. Additional information can be found on the DIDO web page http://dlib.indiana.edu/collections/dido/.

Digital Media and Image Center

The Digital Media and Image Center (DMIC) was established by the Digital Library Program in January 1998 to digitize images, sound, and videorecordings. Imaging for several major grant-funded projects has taken place in the DMIC, including photographs, correspondence, sheet music, lyric sheets, and personal effects from the Hoagy Carmichael Collection housed in the IU Archives of Traditional Music and the University Archives, negatives from the Frank M. Hohenberger Photograph Collection housed in the Lilly Library, and prints from the U.S. Steel Photograph Collection housed in the Calumet Regional Archives at IU-Northwest.

Smaller imaging projects have also been planned and completed in the DMIC, including approximately 600 negatives and prints of the Wylie House, camp manuals documenting procedures of Camp Chickagami for Girls in Winter, Wisconsin, and IU's holdings of the Indiana University Librarians' Association Newsletter in its various forms since 1969.

Staff at the DMIC is also attempting to establish baseline procedures for common types of imaging projects, including resolution requirements, output formats, and quality control procedures. It also provides consulting services for IU departments considering imaging projects. For more information about the DMIC and technical documentation on projects completed there, see the DMIC web page: http://www.dlib.indiana.edu/dmic/.

Current Digital Library Program Projects

Bloomington

Victorian Women Writers Project.

The Victorian Women Writers Project started in 1995, and is devoted to creating electronic editions of works by 19th century British women writers. Women published anthologies, novels, political pamphlets, and volumes of poetry and verse drama, yet it is only now that many of these writers and their works are receiving critical attention. There are currently almost 200 texts available, out of the many thousands to be done, and work is progressing with the help of English Department undergraduate interns. The collection receives an average of 40,000 uses per month. URL: http://www.indiana.edu/~letrs/vwwp/index.html.

Wright American Fiction Project

Nine universities in the Committee on Institutional Cooperation (CIC) are participating on a project to digitize 3,000 works of American fiction published between 1851-1875. This collection is based on Lyle Wright's bibliography American Fiction 1851-1875: a Contribution Toward a Bibliography (San Marino, CA: The Huntington Library, 1965). The titles in this bibliography, including works by Mark Twain, William Dean Howells, Herman Melville, Harriet Beecher Stowe and Louisa May Alcott, will be digitized and made freely available, providing a view of American literature, culture and history of this momentous period. The nine participating libraries are: Indiana University, Michigan State University, The Ohio State University, University of Illinois at Chicago; University of Illinois at Urbana-Champaign; University of Iowa; University of Michigan; University of Minnesota; and University of Wisconsin. URL: http://www.letrs.indiana.edu/web/w/wright2/.

The Indiana University Digital Library Program has received a three-year, United States Department of Education

Title VI Technology Program grant to digitize and offer on the World Wide Web a twenty-year portion of the Letopis' Zhurnal'nykh Statei (1956-1975), a serial publication that indexes Soviet periodicals from 1926 to the present. It covers more than 1,700 journals, series, and continuing publications of academies, universities, and research institutes in the fields of humanities, natural sciences, and the social sciences, and it also covers the popular periodical literature. Once digitized and made available on the World Wide Web, it will provide access to the periodical literature for an essential time in modern Russian history, beginning with the period of the Khrushchev "Thaw" following the 20th CPSU Congress and continuing through the first half of the so-called Brezhnev "Period of Stagnation." For more information: http://www.dlib.indiana.edu/reference/letopis/.

U.S. Steel Photograph Collection

The University received funding from the Indiana State Library/LSTA to digitize the 2,250 photographs in the U.S. Steel Photograph Collection in the Calumet Regional Archive at IU Northwest in Gary for the one-year project. In addition to the photographs the site will feature supplemental texts to provide context for the images and learning activities for students in grades 4-12, developed by Indiana teachers. For more information about the project and sample images: http://www.dlib.indiana.edu/collections/steel/.

Cushman Collection

The University also received a two-year grant from the Institute for Museum and Library Services (IMLS) to digitize and publish on the Web 18,000 slides from the Cushman Collection in the University Archives in Bloomington. This collection includes Kodachrome slides from 1938-1969, which includes a time when few photographers shot color. Mr. Cushman was a highly-skilled amateur photographer who not only photographed people and places around the world, he meticulously documented his work in notebooks. The project continued from October 2000-September 2002. For more information and a sample of the photographs: http://www.dlib.indiana.edu/collections/cushman/.

Digital Music Library

Funding from the National Science Foundation and the National Endowment for the Humanities was received through the Digital Library Initiatives 2 program to create a digital music library. Building upon VARIATIONS, the project aims to establish a digital music library testbed system containing music in a variety of formats, involving research and development in the areas of system architecture, metadata standards, component-based application architecture, and network services. This system will be used as a foundation for digital library research in the areas of instruction, usability, human-computer interaction, and intellectual property rights. The project will run four years, from October 1, 2000-September 30, 2004. For progress reports on the many aspects of the project, see the project web site: http://dml.indiana.edu.

Inscriptions from the Land of Israel

Michael Satlow from the Department of Religious Studies proposes developing a research and demonstration prototype of a web site that presents the material culture of the Land of Israel from the Second Temple period to the Arab conquest (c. 450 BCE – 614 CE). The heart of the site will be the corpus of inscriptions. This prototype will focus on Jerusalem. Both LETRS and the Digital Library Team in Indianapolis are providing support for this project. LETRS is providing e-text and web development; the Indianapolis team is providing map digitization and GIS consultation.

Frank M. Hohenberger Photograph Collection

The University planned and implemented an image digitization project in partnership with the Lilly Library. The first 500 photographs in the Frank M. Hohenberger Photograph Collection have been digitized. A web site for the project offers the complete finding aid, the images, and contextual information about Hohenberger and Brown County. The contextual information includes a biographical essay about Hohenberger written by former Lilly librarian Cecil K. Bryd for an Indiana University Press book of Hohenberger photos and a contemporary article written about Hohenberger and published in the American Magazine in 1933. It is adding subject descriptors to the finding aid in order to increase the consistency of subject searching and continuing to digitize images. URL: http://www.dlib.indiana.edu/collections/lilly/hohenberger/index.html.

Electronic Atlas of Central Indiana

http://atlas.ulib.iupui.edu/

The Atlas is a Web-based repository of maps and GIS (Geographic Information Systems) data covering Central Indiana. The primary goal of the Atlas is to acquire, archive and make available data for the Indianapolis Metropolitan Statistical Area and the nine county region of Boone, Hamilton, Hancock, Hendricks, Johnson, Madison, Marion, Morgan and Shelby counties. The Atlas project is funded by grants from the Indianapolis Foundation. These data include the social and economic data created by the SAVI Project as well as maps and datasets produced by other providers. To date, those providers consist of the U.S. Census Bureau, the U.S. Geological Survey, the IUPUI Center for Earth and Environmental Science, The Polis Center, the United Way of Central Indiana and the Natural Resource Conservation Service. Maps are currently available as images (PDF files which allow some limited interaction with the data) and as downloadable files (for experts who want to manipulate the data on their own computers).

The Atlas encompasses several digital library initiatives including Geographic Information Systems development, the Historical Aerial Archive, the Indiana Geographic Information Catalog, and Historical Maps.

Geographic Information Systems

An object oriented spatial database is under development. The system will facilitate the development of an online mapping system. The retrieval and delivery system being developed for the Atlas will also provide a dynamic data download and decompression application.

Historical Aerial Archive

http://atlas.ulib.iupui.edu/aerials/

Digitized historical aerial photographs of six of the nine counties of Central Indiana have been incorporated into the Atlas. An image server allows users to pan or zoom on the image. Future enhancements will include address-matching capabilities.

Historical Maps

Funded in part by the Ayres Foundation, the Historical Maps section of the Atlas will include a selection of maps from Indianapolis and the Central Indiana region. The team has consulted with the Indiana State Library, the Indiana State Museum, and the IU Geography and Map Library on the project.

Indiana Geographic Information Catalog

http://in-ulib-brayton.ads.iu.edu/MetadataExplorer/

The development of the catalog is funded in part by a grant from the Federal Geographic Data Committee of the US Geological Survey. Metadata records from local and state agencies are being added to the catalog. These metadata records contain information about geo-spatial data created within the State and that data's location. The catalog will eventually be connected to the National Geospatial Data Clearinghouse, http://130.11.52.184/, operated by the Federal Geographic Data Committee.

IUPUI University Libraries Community Project: in Collaboration with Central Indiana Schools, Museums, and Public Libraries http://www.ulib.iupui.edu/imls/home.html

Funded by a National Leadership Grant from the Institute of Museum and Library Services (IMLS), IUPUI University Library offers access to digital image databases to public libraries and K-12 educational institutions. The Indianapolis Museum of Art has joined IUPUI University Library as the main supporting partner on the Community Project whose purpose is to enrich the lives of members of the community through visual arts. Other museum supporters of the Community Project are The Eiteljorg Museum of American Indians and Western Art, The Indiana State Museum, The Children's Museum, and The Indiana Historical Society.

Philanthropic Studies Index

http://cheever.ulib.iupui.edu/psipublicsearch/

The Philanthropic Studies Index (PSI) is an online reference tool to literature on voluntarism, nonprofit organizations, fundraising, and charitable giving. PSI, for the present, provides access to periodical articles, both current and retrospective. In the future, coverage will increase to include relevant books, dissertations, working papers, and other information sources relevant to the ever-growing field of philanthropy. PSI covers 1940 to 1999. PSI was migrated into an Oracle database structure in 2000. A web interface for citation editing and data loading have been incorporated into the management system. Future enhancements will include development of advanced searching functionality, development of new data entry screens, and gathering and delivery of detailed search statistics.

New Digital Library Initiatives

Integrating Access to Electronic Resources. The Digital Library Program will work with others in the IU Libraries, at IUB and IUPUI and elsewhere in the university, toward the goal of integrating existing electronic resources into a more comprehensive and accessible source. These currently include full text reference sources (Encyclopedia Britannica, OED), bibliographic indexes (Expanded Academic Index), and full text journals (MUSE, JSTOR and some journals within EAI). Each of these resources looks and works differently; the University needs to plan to get these resources to work together better.

Digital Library Research. Indian University proposes three areas of research: (i) digital libraries as complex (technological, social, organizational and human) systems; (ii) streaming audio and video data as digital library services; and (iii) the relation of testbed digital libraries to networked learning environments and collaborative work spaces. The proposed electronic reserve system above offers but one set of digital library opportunities. Research focusing on the electronic reserve project could advance the state of knowledge and practice in digital libraries through the contributions of IU's research faculty in areas of human-computer interaction and systems design, instructional systems technology, social and organizational informatics, and others. Other areas with research potential include innovative user services, digital collections management, digital library system design, and streaming media.

Streaming Digital Media. The Digital Library Program will undertake a program of research and development in the network delivery of audio and video content, for example: IP-video and IP-audio, Quality of Service, and network infrastructure; user interaction and usability; metadata for discovery and retrieval of video and audio; scaleability; authentication and intellectual property; security; other technology issues. This work will build on IU's experience in delivering networked audio and video library services (through the Variations Project and the IMDS-Interactive Media Distribe to explore with the Indiana University a project to digitize their entire database of documentary films and license it to academic institutions. This project would have potential on a number of levels, serving both the academic community and the distributors of documentary films. It would give Indiana

University a unique opportunity to explore the necessary technology to provide this service. It would also lend itself to an interesting program of research. It would have a testbed for a number of business models related to distributing a "full-text database" of moving images and would hope to gain valuable information about how students and faculty use networked motion pictures.

Network Access to Unique Collections. The Digital Library Program will undertake projects to provide network access to digitized resources — specialized texts, rare books and manuscripts, ephemeral or pre-publication literature, and other texts and artifacts from the collections of the IU Libraries.

Digital Library Seminar Series. The Digital Library Program will offer a seminar series, highlighting issues related to digital libraries. Some of the seminars will be offered over the lunch hour once a month. Others will be larger and use national speakers, perhaps twice a year. We will also explore the possibility of sponsoring a national teleconference, similar to Networked Information and the Scholar (October 1994). This teleconference would bring together digital library experts from a number of fields. The purposes of the seminar series are (1) to increase knowledge about digital libraries throughout Indiana University; and (2) to increase the visibility of Indiana University as an international participant in digital library developments.

Infrastructure for Digital Libraries

Inter-institutional Collaboration.

The Digital Library Program will collaborate with colleagues at other colleges, universities, and research libraries in the development of an inter-institutional and international federation of distributed digital libraries. Special emphasis will be given to long-standing collaborative partners, such as institutional members of the CIC, and through partnerships within the Digital Library Federation of which IU is a member. These collaborations will take the form of digitization projects, such as the Wright American Fiction Project, software development, such as with the University of Virginia on FEDORA, and Perry Willett's work on TEI guidelines.

Digital Library Architecture and Infrastructure

The Digital Library Program will develop and help implement a common architecture for digital libraries at IU. The DLP will advise or directly support individual centers devoted to creating and managing digital collections or delivering networked information services, and will seek to integrate these into a common design architecture that is scaleable, sustainable, and interoperable. University Information Technology Services (UITS) will develop and deliver technology infrastructure services in support of the DLP: campus and wide-area networking, data center operations and management, application design and development, or others. UITS and SLIS can provide support for user requirements analysis, user-centered design, and usability testing. The Advanced Information Technology Laboratory (AITL) in UITS will provide technology assessment, evaluation and testbed development in support of the DLP.

Consultation and Advisory Services

The Digital Library Program cannot directly guide or manage every project in the wide array of digital library services that will be developed and implemented at Indiana University. For projects not under its direct guidance, the role of DLP is to provide advice and consultation as requested regarding the direction taken by such digital collections and services and to help assure their integration with other digital library services and with the IU digital library architecture. The Digital Library Program staff will work with Library Information Technology and other units to delineate specific areas of responsibility. They will also develop a plan for communicating their services throughout the university.

12
Digital Library Projects in the Australian Universities

Australia is supporting digital library projects at the national, state and university levels together with commercial and research issues. An overview is provided below of some of the current projects with attempt to give an insight into the issues being addressed to there. Only a few leading projects have been taken up for discussion and there may be many more others like them.

The institutions which have undertaken the projects mainly include Monash University, University of Queensland, Queensland University of Technology, Griffith University, University of Central Queensland, Southern Cross University, the Australian Catholic University, University of Sydney, Curtin University, Murdoch University, the Centre for Development Studies at Edith Cowan University and the Inter-University Consortium for Development Studies, Edith Cowan University, Curtin University of Technology and, the University of Western Australia.

Electronic Reserve Project

Monash University is one of the most reputed institutions of Australia. For the purpose of digitization a new branch of its Library was opened in March 1996. It contains four banks of computers and there are virtually no books on the shelves. It reflects the University's declared intention to create an electronic campus at Berwick and to provide library facilities by electronic delivery (however there is back-up from a conventional library located on the adjacent Casey TAFE campus.) The electronic reserve collection is at the core of the "electronic library" at Berwick. Students may retrieve, view and print bit-mapped images of journal articles, book chapters and similar recommended course readings. There are now more than 400 items in this rapidly growing "collection". The existing arrangements require the Library to approach publishers for each item separately requesting approval to scan and store the item in digital format. In the majority of cases, publishers have given this approval without charging a royalty fee.

The system resides on a Windows NT server. The viewer software for the project was developed in the Library. Multi-page TIFF Images are accessed via a WWW front end to the Library Catalogue on which records for all imaged documents are created. Users may click on a hot link to view the image of the document.

Electronic Journal Project

In 1995, Australia made a research grant to Monash University Library to conduct a pilot project in the transfer of an existing conventional journal, the Australasian Journal of Engineering Education (AJEE), to electronic media. The project involves the University Library, the Unit of Medical Informatics, and the UNESCO-supported International Centre for Engineering Education (USICEE), in the Faculty of Engineering. During 1995, the appropriate hardware and software were acquired to serve as the host for the project and for future electronic publishing ventures. A staff member from the Library was trained in the various skills required in creating information for distribution via the World Wide Web. Three electronic issues of the journal (volume 6, numbers 1 and 2, and volume 7, no. 1) have been published to date in parallel with the paper versions and made available for viewing on the World Wide Web. Reader comments were obtained by means of a questionnaire sent to all subscribers.

A further research grant of $30,000 was provided by the

University from its 1996 Quality Funds. This will enable the project team to continue to publish all issues of the AJEE electronically on the World Wide Web, using the techniques that have been pioneered during 1995. Procedures for the electronic submission, reviewing, refereeing and editing of all manuscripts to the AJEE will be developed and trialled. Alternative methods for the processing of electronic subscriptions, including the collection of subscription fees, using electronic payment software, credit card secure on- line transactions, micro-billing for specific information visited, etc. will be investigated and trialled. Expansion of the scope of the publishing venture will be explored with the editors of other scholarly journals that are published by or under the auspices of Monash University faculties and departments.

REDD: An Electronic Document Delivery Project

REDD is a "first" for Australia - an electronic document delivery system which uses a World Wide Web (WWW) browser, Multipurpose Internet Mail Extension (MIME), e-mail and Common Gateway Interface (CGI) programs to electronically transmit requests for documents and the documents themselves between users. It is a hardware independent solution that does not necessitate the purchase or use of vendor specific software on each user's workstation.

REDD was developed by The University of Queensland, Queensland University of Technology and Griffith University Libraries to meet the need for a fast, inexpensive and accessible electronic document delivery infrastructure for Australia. The project received seed funding from the Australian Research Council's 1994 Research Infrastructure (Equipment and Facilities) Programme.

Registered REDD users access an electronic request form on their library's World Wide Web server, fill in their personal and bibliographic details, and send the completed request form to their local library. Interlibrary loans staff in the local library edit the form and then send it to the selected supplying library. The supplying library then retrieves the requested item, scans it and emails it to the requesting library. At this stage, the requesting library prints the item for the requester. The implications of sending scanned items direct to the user's workstation are under investigation.

Currently, REDD is being used by staff, students and document delivery staff at eight institutions: The University of Queensland, Queensland University of Technology, Griffith University, the University of Southern Queensland, University of Central Queensland, Southern Cross University, the Australian Catholic University and the State Library of New South Wales.

Hume Image Collection Project

The University of Queensland's Hume collection consists of a rare collection of photographic prints that capture the life of the Hume family, a leading Queensland pastoral family, between 1870 and 1890. The collection is a primary research resource on the development of Queensland's Darling Downs area and is unique, in heavy demand, and largely inaccessible due to its fragility.

Photographs were described, scanned, and compressed using JPEG compression at 25:1 compression ratio. CGI scripts were written to integrate text and image files. Files were then stored and made available via the Library's web server. Testing is still under way and public access to the database should be available via the Library's home page by January 1997.

DIGILIB: Queensland Country Towns Image Project

The Queensland Country Towns Database (DIGILIB) is a collaborative project between The University of Queensland's Architecture Department and Library. Stage 1 of the project involved using a broadcast quality video camera to digitise one thousand colour slides, compressing these using JPEG compression at 25:1 compression ratio, and storing the data on the Library's file server. Each image was described and a

MARC-based proforma developed to guide the descriptive process.

The slides focus on Queensland historic buildings ranging from domestic, public, mining, and agricultural buildings, many of which have now been demolished. As a number of the buildings have not been recorded elsewhere, the collection is significant as a record of the nation's cultural heritage and is a heavily-used teaching, learning and research resource.

Stage 2 involved transferring the text and image files created in stage 1 to a format suitable for the World Wide Web. The Web- based product allows both simple searching and advanced searching where users can select multiple combinations of terms. There are also a number of ways in which records retrieved can be viewed. The database is still under development with plans to incorporate Quicktime VR and enable searching by image shape as well as traditional text based searching.

Australian Cooperative Digitisation Project 1840-45

This project will create a unique research infrastructure in Australian studies through the digital conversion of Australian serials and fiction of the seminal period 1840-45. The project will ensure access to and preservation of this material by a process of microfilming, scanning, and networking. The first project of its kind in Australia, it will introduce international best practice, act as a technical benchmark, and provide a new level of resource sharing. This Commonwealth Australian Research Council funded project is a national collaborative project between the University of Sydney Library (project leader), the State Library of New South Wales, the National Library of Australia, and Monash University Library.

The project will work through several stages. These are: selection of items, conservation preparation of items, preservation microfilming to Australian and international standards, preservation digitisation of microfilm to TIFF image files, conversion of selected microfilm to ASCII text, design and implementation of document control structure and interface, design and provision of network delivery system (including compression), documentation and training, and preservation storage of microfilm masters and master digital data files.

Scholarly Electronic Text and Image Service

SETIS is the Scholarly Electronic Text and Image Service at the University of Sydney. Located in and operated by the University Library, SETIS aims to exploit fully the latest developments in information technology for students and scholars, particularly within the arts and humanities.

Modeled on similar centres in the United Kingdom and the United States of America, and particularly the highly successful Electronic Text Center at the University of Virginia, SETIS is the first service of its kind in Australia. SETIS aims, therefore, to be in a position to provide a leadership and advisory role for similar developments in our region.

In addition to providing networked access to commercial electronic texts such as the English Poetry Full-Text Database, the Bible in English, the Intelex Past Masters philosophy texts and many more, SETIS also provides access to textual analysis software, electronic text creation software and equipment, and the necessary training and support required for these.

The skills developed at SETIS will allow the University Library to support the creation of electronic versions of public domain texts at the university and their dissemination throughout the World Wide Web. The collection of freely available texts will be significant because SETIS will be the Asia-Pacific mirror site for the substantial collection of electronic texts maintained at the University of Virginia.

UNILINC Projects

UNILINC is a non-profit cooperative of higher education and related libraries in Australia and has several electronic journal projects. UNILINC has mounted two electronic journal databases (ABI/Inform and Periodical Research 11) which together deliver over 1000 electronic journals to the desktop. In addition, OVID's Core Biomedical Research (CBC)1 collection has been mounted and CBC2 will soon be made available. These collections comprise the fulltext including graphics of some 22 core journals. They are linked by keys in the Medline and other NLM databases available via OVID. These fulltext databases are additional to another 16 citation and abstract databases available online.

The participating libraries encourage full use by undergraduates as well as academics and researchers from within the library, the university network and from home. UNILINC will be putting up further electronic journal collections as they become available.

In addition to database services, UNILINC has a Shared Library System, CD-CAT (the first CD ROM produced in Australia and at its 24th edition and using software developed in Australia), a cooperative purchasing program for online and CD ROM databases and a contract cataloguing service.

LISWEB Project

The LISWEB project provides Curtin University clients with information about the library services, tells them what can be done for them, and offers easy access to quality sources of scholarly information. It also includes at least three innovative features.

1. **Interactive Information Literacy.** The WWW offers an excellent platform to make the core of our existing information literacy program available to students world-wide, irrespective of place or time. Skills enhancement programs on the WWW offer media-rich materials which can be explored in an interactive mode. The core literacy content for Health Sciences is currently offered, and content will be expanded to other subject areas later this year.

2. **Exam papers.** Students use exam papers as a major and valued information resource. These have been scanned in for the past three years and made them available through LISWEB.
3. **EasySearch.** In an increasingly web-centric environment, clients expect to be able to access catalogues and other databases through the WWW. DRAWEB, a commercial product, has been substantially enhanced by, for example, adding a Boolean "and" feature to meet these client needs.

Indian Ocean Rim Region Virtual Library Project

The Indian Ocean Rim Region Virtual Library Project has been jointly developed by Edith Cowan and Murdoch University Libraries, the Centre for Development Studies at Edith Cowan University and the Inter-University Consortium for Development Studies Western Australia (comprising Edith Cowan University, Murdoch University, Curtin University of Technology and, the University of Western Australia). The project is a co-operative venture initially focusing on Social Development, including health issues, in the Indian Ocean Rim Region.

The aims of the project are to:

* Connect researchers and developmental organisations within the region
* Provide accessible information in electronic format
* Contribute to a network for the dissemination of information
* Foster and support the exchange of information
* Provide better access to data for researchers and students in the region who may be isolated

Social development has been defined as a process of change which involves the interaction of political, economic, social, production, technological, international and administrative systems. More specifically, social development in the contemporary world focuses on social issues such as Health, Economic and Social Development, Environmental Issues, Economy, Education, Gender, Ethnicity, Indigenous Groups and Labour.

Bibliography

Alan Bundy. *A window of opportunity: libraries and learning in the 21st century*, paper presented at the Australian Library and Information Association Distance Education Special Interest Group Conference "Flexible Learning - the new paradigm", Monash University, 13 - 14 February 2000, <*http://www.library.unisa.edu.au/papers/window.htm*>.

Allen Brewer, Wei Ding, Karla Hahn, and Anita Komlodi. The Role of Intermediary Services in Emerging Digital Libraries. In *Proceedings of DL'96*, 1996.

Amarnath Gupta, Bertram Ludaescher, and Reagan W. Moore. *Ontology Services for Curriculum Development in NSDL.* In *Proceedings of the Second ACM/IEEE-CS Joint Conference on Digital Libraries*, 2002.

American Library Association, *A Progress Report on Information Literacy: An Update on the American Library Association Presidential Committee on Information Literacy: Final Report*, 1998, <*http://www.ala.org/acrl/nili/nili.html*>.

Amjad Ali. Digital libraries in the making. New Delhi, Ess Ess Publications, 2005.

Amjad Ali. Information technology and libraries. New Delhi, Ess Ess Publications, 2004.

Amjad Ali. Learning in the information age. New Delhi, Ess Ess Publications, 2004.

Amjad Ali. Reference service and the digital sources of information. New Delhi, Ess Ess Publications, 2004.

Anderson, Elizabeth, et. al. Digitizing Legacy Documents: A Knowledge-Based Preservation Project. Fermi National Accelerator Laboratory, September 1998.

Anderson, Eric, Josh Boyer, and Karen Ciccone. Remote reference services at the North Carolina State University Libraries. Paper presented at Facets of Digital Reference Service: The Virtual Reference Desk Second Annual Digital Reference Conference, October 16-17, 2000. *http://www.vrd.org/conferences/VRD2000/proceedings/boyer-anderson-ciccone12-14.shtml*

Andy Dong and Alice M. Agogino. Design Principles for the Information Architecture of a SMET Education Digital Library. In *Proceedings of the First ACM/IEEE-CS Joint Conference on Digital Libraries*, 2001.

Ann Blandford, Hanna Stelmaszewska, and Nick Bryan-Kinns. Use of Multiple Digital Libraries: A Case Study. In *Proceedings of the First ACM/IEEE-CS Joint Conference on Digital Libraries*, 2001.

Ann Peterson Bishop. Making Digital Libraries Go: Comparing Use Across Genres. In *Proceedings of the Fourth ACM International Conference on Digital Libraries*, 1999.

Arts and Humanities Data Service. A Strategic Policy Framework for Creating and Preserving Digital Collections. October 23, 1995. URL: *http://ahds.ac.uk/manage/framework.htm*

Arts and Humanities Data Service. A Strategic Policy Framework for Creating and Preserving Digital Collections. October 23, 1995.

Arturo Crespo and Hector Garcia-Molina. *Archival Storage for Digital Libraries.* In *Proceedings of the Third ACM International Conference on Digital Libraries,* 1998. Accessible at http://dbpubs.stanford.edu/pub/1998-49.

Arturo Crespo and Hector Garcia-Molina. *Routing Indices For*

Peer-to-Peer Systems. Number 2001-48. Stanford University, 2001.

Association of Research Libraries. Definition and Purposes of a Digital Library. October 23, 1995. URL: *http://www.ifla.org/documents/libraries/net/arl-dlib.txt*

Association of Research Libraries. Definition and Purposes of a Digital Library. October 23, 1995.

Augusto Celentano and others. Knowledge-Based Document Retrieval in Office Environments: The Kabiria System. *ACM Transactions on Information Systems*, 13(3):237-268, July, 1995.

B. Amento, L. Terveen, and W. Hill. Does authority mean quality? Predicting expert quality ratings of web documents. In *Proceedings of the Twenty-Third Annual International ACM SIGIR Conference on Research and Development in Information Retrieval*. ACM, 2000.

Bernardo A. Huberman and Lada A. Adamic. Growth dynamics of the World-Wide Web. *Nature*, 401(6749), September, 1999.

Boris Chidlovskii, Claudia Roncancio, and Marie-Luise Schneider. Semantic Cache Mechanism for Heterogeneous Web Querying. In *Proceedings of the Eighth International World-Wide Web Conference*, 1999.

Brian Cooper and Hector Garcia-Molina. *Bidding for storage space in a peer-to-peer data preservation system*. Number 2001-52. Stanford University, 2001.

Brian Cooper and Hector Garcia-Molina. *Bidding for storage space in a peer-to-peer data preservation system (Extended version)*. Number 2002-22. Stanford University, 2002.

Brian Cooper and Hector Garcia-Molina. Creating Trading Networks of Digital Archives. In *Proceedings of the First ACM/IEEE-CS Joint Conference on Digital Libraries*, 2001.

Brian Cooper, Mayank Bawa, Neil Daswani, and Hector Garcia-

Molina. *Protecting the PIPE from malicious peers.* Number 2002-97. Stanford University, 2002.

Brian Cooper, Mayank Bawa, Neil Daswani, and Hector Garcia-Molina. *Protecting the PIPE from malicious peers.* Number 2002-03. Stanford University, 2002..

Brian Kahin. *Institutional and Policy Issues in the Development of the Digital Library.* In *JEP*, 1994.

C. Faloutsos and D. Oard. *A Survey of Information Retrieval and Filtering Methods.* Dept. of Computer Science, University of Maryland, 1995.

C. Mic Bowman, Peter B. Danzig, Darren R. Hardy, Udi Manber, Michael F. Schwartz, and Duane P. Wessels. *Harvest: A Scalable, Customizable Discovery and Access System.* Number CU-CS-732-94. Dept. of Computer Science, Univ. of Colorado, Boulder, Colo. August, 1994. Accessible at http://harvest.transarc.com/.

C.M. Bowman, Peter B. Danzig, Darren R. Hardy, Udi Manber, and Michael F. Schwartz. The Harvest information discovery and access system. *Computer Networks and ISDN Systems*, 28(1-2):119-125, December, 1995.

Carol Ann Hughes, "Information Services for Higher Education. A New Competitive Space," *D-Lib Magazine*, December 2000, *<http://www.dlib.org/dlib/december00/hughes/12hughes.html>*.

Carol Collier Kuhltau, "Student learning in the library; what Library Power librarians say," *School Libraries Worldwide*, 5(2), 1999.

Carol Twigg and Michael Miloff, "The global learning infrastructure," in: Don Tapscott, Alex Lowry and David Ticoll, *Blueprint to the digital economy*, McGraw-Hill, 1998.

Charles Anderson. Reference librarianship: a guide for the 21st century. The Reference Librarian, Number 72, 5-19. 2001.

Charles Kacmar, Dean Jue, David Stage, and Christie Koontz.

Automatic Creation and Maintenance of an Organizational Spatial Metadata and Document Digital Library. In *Proceedings of the Second Annual Conference on the Theory and Practice of Digital Libraries*, 1995.

Chen-Chuan K. Chang, Héctor García-Molina, and Andreas Paepcke. *Boolean Query Mapping Across Heterogeneous Information Sources (Extended Version)*. Number Christine L. Borgman, Gregory Leazer, Anne Gilliland-Swetland, Kelli Millwood, Leslie Champeny, Jason Finley, and Laura J. Smart. How Geography Professors Select Materials for Classroom Lectures: Implications for the Design of Digital Libraries. In *Proceedings of the Fourth ACM/IEEE-CS Joint Conference on Digital Libraries*, 2004.

Daniel V Pitti. The Berkeley Finding Aid Project: Standards in Navigation. University of California, Berkeley. URL: *http://www.ifla.org/documents/libraries/net/pitd1.txt*

David Gibson, Jon M. Kleinberg, and Prabhakar Raghavan. Inferring Web Communities from Link Topology. In *HyperText*, 1998.

David Hawking, Nick Craswell, Paul Thistlewaite, and Donna Harman. Results and Challenges in Web Search Evaluation. In *Proceedings of the Eighth International World-Wide Web Conference*, 1999.

David J Harper, Sara Coluthard, Raja Kalpana, and Sun Yixing. *A Language Modelling Approach to Relevance Profiling for Document Browsing*. In *Proceedings of the Second ACM/IEEE-CS Joint Conference on Digital Libraries*, 2002.

Digital Preservation Consortium. Mission and Goals. March 1994. URL: *http://www.ifla.org/documents/libraries/net/dpc1.txt*

Don Waters. Electronic Technologies and Preservation. Based on a Presentation to the Annual Meeting of the Research Libraries Group, June 25, 1992. URL: *http://www.ifla.org/documents/libraries/net/waters1.txt*

Donald Beagle, "Web-based learning environments: do libraries matter," *College & Research Libraries*, 61 (4), July 2000.

Doug Cutting, Bill Janssen, Mike Spreitzer, and Farrell Wymore. *ILU Reference Manual*. Xerox Palo Alto Research Center, December, 1993. Accessible at ftp: / /ftp.parc.xerox.com/ pub/ilu/ ilu.html.

Douglass R. Cutting, David Karger, and Jan Pedersen. Constant interaction-time Scatter/Gather browsing of very large document collections. In *Proceedings of the Sixteenth Annual International ACM SIGIR Conference on Research and Development in Information Retrieval*, pp. 126-135, 1993.

Edward Chang and Hector Garcia-Molina. *Cost-Based Media Server Design*. In *To appear in the proceedings of the 8th Research Issues in Data Engineering*, Feb, 1998.

Edward Chang and Hector Garcia-Molina. Effective Memory Use in a Media Server. In *Proceedings of the 23rd Very Large Data Base (VLDB) Conference*, 1997.

Edward Galloway A. and V. Michalek Gabrielle. The Heinz Electronic Library Interactive Online System (HELIOS): Building a Digital Archive Using Imaging, OCR, and Natural Language Processing Technologies. The Public-Access Computer Systems Review 6, no. 4 (1995). URL: *http://www.ifla.org/documents/libraries/net/gale1.txt*

Elizabeth Anderson, et. al. Digitizing Legacy Documents: A Knowledge-Based Preservation Project. Fermi National Accelerator Laboratory, September 1998. PDF: *http://www.ifla.org/documents/libraries/net/tm-2056.pdf*

Elke Dunker. *Cross-cultural Usability of the Library Metaphor*. In *Proceedings of the Second ACM/IEEE-CS Joint Conference on Digital Libraries*, 2002.

Eric Bier, Lance Good, Kris Popat, and Alan Newberger. A Document Corpus Browser for In-Depth Reading. In

Proceedings of the Fourth ACM/IEEE-CS Joint Conference on Digital Libraries, 2004.

Eric H. Johnson and Pauline A. Cochrane. *A Hypertextual Interface for a Searcher's Thesaurus*. In *Proceedings of the Second Annual Conference on the Theory and Practice of Digital Libraries*, 1995.

Eric W. Brown, James P. Callan, and W. Bruce Croft. Fast Incremental Indexing for Full-Text Information Retrieval. In *Proceedings of the Twentieth Internationl Conference on Very Large Databases*, pp. 192-202, September, 1994.

Fabio Crestani. Vocal Access to a Newspaper Archive: Design Issues and Preliminary Investigations. In *Proceedings of the Fourth ACM International Conference on Digital Libraries*, 1999.

Francine Chen, Marti Hearst, Julian Kupiec, Jan Pedersen, and Lynn Wilcox. *Mixed-Media Access*. In *Proceedings of the First Annual Conference on the Theory and Practice of Digital Libraries*, 1994.

Frank M. Shipman III, Haowei Hsieh, J. Michael Moore, and Anna Zacchi. Supporting Personal Collections across Digital Libraries in Spatial Hypertext. In *Proceedings of the Fourth ACM/IEEE-CS Joint Conference on Digital Libraries*, 2004.

Frank Wattenberg, "A National Digital Library for Science, Mathematics, Engineering and Technology Education," *D-Lib Magazine*, October 1998, <*http://www.dlib.org/dlib/october98/wattenberg/10wattenberg.html*>.

Frankie James. AHA: Audio HTML Access. In Michael R. Genesereth and Anna Patterson, editors, *Proceedings of the Sixth International World Wide Web Conference. Published in Computer Networks and ISDN Systems, vol.29, no.8-13, p.1395-404, 0169-7552 Elsevier Sept. 1997*, pp. 129-140. IW3C, Santa Clara, CA, April, 1997.

Frankie James. *Distinguishability vs. Distraction in Audio*

HTML Interfaces. In *Submitted to International Journal on Digital Libraries*, 1997.

Franz J. Hauck. Supporting hierarchical guided tours in the WorldWideWeb. In *Proceedings of the Fifth International World-Wide Web Conference*, 1996.

Fred Douglis, Anja Feldmann, and Balachander Krishnamurthy. Rate of Change and other metrics: a Live Study of the World Wide Web. In *USENIX Symposium on Internetworking Technologies and Systems*, 1999.

Fred Douglis, Antonio Haro, and Michael Rabinovich. HPP: HTML Macro-Preprocessing to Support Dynamic Document Caching. In *Proceedings of the USENIX Symposium on Internet Technologies and Systems, Monterey, California*, 1997.

Fred Douglis, Thomas Ball, Yih-Farn Chen, and Eleftherios Koutsofios. WebGUIDE: Querying and Navigating Changes in Web Repositories. In *Proceedings of the Fifth International World-Wide Web Conference*, May, 1996.

Fred Douglis, Thomas Ball, Yih-Farn Chen, and Eleftherios Koutsofios. The AT&T Internet Difference Engine: Tracking and Viewing Changes on the Web. *World Wide Web*, 1(1):27-44, January, 1998.

Fred Friedman, Arthur M. Keller, Gio Wiederhold, Mike R. Berkowitz, John Salasin, and David L. Spooner. Reference Model for ADA Interfaces to Database Management Systems. In *Proceedings Second IEEE Computer Society Data Engineering Conference*, 1986.

Fred M Hayward, Internationalization of U.S. Higher Education: Preliminary Status Report, American Council on Education (Washington, DC, 2000)

G. W. Fitzmaurice. Situated information spaces and spatially aware palmtop computers. *Communications of the ACM*, 36(7):38-49, Jul, 1993.

Gary Geisler, Sarah Giersch, David McArthur, and Marty McClelland. *Creating Virtual Collections in Digital*

Libraries: Benefits and Implementation Issues. In *Proceedings of the Second ACM/IEEE-CS Joint Conference on Digital Libraries*, 2002.

Gary King, H. T. Kung, Barbara Grosz, Sidney Verba, Dale Flecker, and Brian Kahin. *The Harvard Self-Enriching Library Facilities (SELF) Project.* In *Proceedings of the First Annual Conference on the Theory and Practice of Digital Libraries*, 1994.

George W. Furnas. Generalized Fisheye Views. In *Proceedings of the Conference on Human Factors in Computing Systems CHI'86*, 1986.

Gregor Kiczales and Andreas Paepcke. *Open Implementations and Metaobject Protocols.* 1994. Expanded tutorial notes. At http://db.stanford.edu/ paepcke/shared-documents/Tutorial.ps.

Gregory B Newby. The Digital Electronic Library. January 29, 1991. URL: *http://www.ifla.org/documents/libraries/net/newby.txt*

Gregory Crane, Clifford E. Wulfman, Lisa M. Cerrato, Anne Mahoney, Thomas L. Milbank, David Mimno, Jeffrey A. Rydberg-Cox, David A. Smith, and Christopher

Gregory Crane. Building a Digital Library: The Perseus Project as a Case Study in the Humanities. In *Proceedings of DL'96*, 1996.

Hannelore B. Rader, "Educating students for the information age: the role of the librarian," *Reference Services Review*, 25(2), Summer 1997.

Hannelore B. Rader, "Faculty-librarian collaboration in building the curriculum for the millennium: the US experience," *IFLA Journal*, 25(4), 1999.

Hans Roes, "Digital libraries and the changing world of education," paper presented at the Thessaloniki Spring Course on the Digital Library, Thessaloniki 23 - 28 May 1999, <*http://cwis.kub.nl/~dbi/users/roes/articles/dlibeduc.htm*>.

Hector Garcia-Molina, Steven Ketchpel, and Narayanan Shivakumar. *Safeguarding and Charging for Information on the Internet.* In *Proceedings of the Fourteenth International Conference on Data Engineering*, 1998. Available at http: / / dbpubs.stanford.edu / pub / 1998-26.

Herb Becker. The Role of the Library of Congress in the National Digital Library. In *Proceedings of DL'96*, 1996.

ISO. *ISO 8777:1993 Information and Documentation - Commands for Interactive Text Searching.* Int'l Organization for Standardization, First, Geneva, Switzerland, 1993.

J. Frew, M. Aurand, B. Buttenfield, L. Carver, P. Chang, R. Ellis, C. Fischer, M. Gardner, M. Goodchild, G. Hajic, M. Larsgaard, K. Park, M. Probert, T. Smith, and Q. Zheng. The Alexandria Rapid Prototype: Building A Digital Library for Spatial Information. In *Advances in Digital Libraries '95*, 1995.

James Davis, and Carl Lagoze. Dienst, A Protocol for a Distributed Digital Document Library. URL: *http://www.broadcatch.com/dienst.html*

James W. Cooper, Mahesh Viswanathan, Donna Byron, and Margaret Chan. Building Searchable Collections of Enterprise Speech Data. In *Proceedings of the First ACM/IEEE-CS Joint Conference on Digital Libraries*, 2001.

Jane Hunter and Sharmin Choudhury. A Semi-Automated Digital Preservation System based on Semantic Web Services. In *Proceedings of the Fourth ACM/IEEE-CS Joint Conference on Digital Libraries*, 2004.

Jessica Albano. Digital Reference Report. University of Washington Libraries. August 1, 1999. *http://faculty.washington.edu/jalbano/digref/*

John Barnard, "The World Wide Web and higher education: the promise of virtual universities and online libraries," *Educational technology*, 37(3), May - June 1997.

John Buford. Evaluation of a Query Language for Structured HyperMedia Documents. In *DAGS '95*. 1995.

John Garrett. Digital Libraries: The Grand Challenges. EDUCOM Review, July/August 1993, Volume 28, Number 4. URL: *http://www.ifla.org/documents/libraries/net/garrett.txt*

John Seely Brown and Paul Duguid, *The social life of information*, Harvard Business School Press, 2000.

Jonathan T. Hujsak. *Digital Libraries and Corporate Technology Reuse. D-Lib Magazine*, Jan, 1996.

José-Marie Griffiths and Kimberly K. Kertis. *Access to Large Digital Libraries of Scientific Information Across Networks*. In *Proceedings of the First Annual Conference on the Theory and Practice of Digital Libraries*, 1994.

Judith Edwards. *The Electronic World and Central Queensland University*. In *Proceedings of the First Annual Conference on the Theory and Practice of Digital Libraries*, 1994.

Junghoo Cho and Hector Garcia-Molina. *Estimating Frequency of Change*. In *submitted for publication*, 2000. Available at http://dbpubs.stanford.edu/pub/2000-4.

Kate Ehrlich and Debra Cash. *Turning Information into Knowledge: Information Finding as a Collaborative Activity*. In *Proceedings of the First Annual Conference on the Theory and Practice of Digital Libraries*, 1994.

Kathleen M. Flynn. *The Knowledge Manager as a Digital Librarian: An Overview of the Knowledge Management Pilot Program at the MITRE Corporation*. In *Proceedings of the Second Annual Conference on the Theory and Practice of Digital Libraries*, 1995.

Kersten Fridén, "The librarian as a teacher: experiences from a problem-based setting," *Health Libraries Review*, 13, 1996.

L. Francis. Mobile computing-a fact in your future. In *15th Annual International Conference on Computer*

Documentation Conference Proceedings. SIGDOC '97. Crossroads in Communication, pp. 63-7, 1997.

Laura M. Bartolo, Cathy S. Lowe, Adam C. Powell IV, Donald R. Sadoway, Jorges Vieyra, and Kyle Stemen. Use of MatML with Software Applications for E-learning. In *Proceedings of the Fourth ACM/IEEE-CS Joint Conference on Digital Libraries*,

Lee L. Zia, "The NSF national science, mathematics, engineering, and technology education digital library (NSDL) program," *D-Lib Magazine*, October 2000, <*http://www.dlib.org/dlib/october00/zia/10zia.html*

Leonard N. Foner. Clustering and Information Sharing in an Ecology of Cooperating Agents. In *AAAI Spring Symposium on Information Gathering*, 1995.

Leslie Bondaryk. *Calculus Modules OnLine: An Internet Multimedia Application.* In *DAGS'95*, 1995.

Leslie Champeny, Christine L. Borgman, Patricia Mautone, Richard E. Mayer, Richard A. Johnson, Gregory H. Leazer, Anne J. Gilliland-Swetland, Kelli A. Millwood, Leonard D'Avolio, Jason Finley, and Laura J. Smart. Developing a Digital Learning Environment: an evaluation of design and implementation processes. In *Proceedings of the Fourth ACM/IEEE-CS Joint Conference on Digital Libraries*, 2004.

Lian-Heong Chua, Dion Hoe-Lian Goh, Ee-Peng Lim, Zehua Liu, and Rebecca Pei-Hui Ang. *A Digital Library For Geography Examination Resources.* In *Proceedings of the Second ACM/IEEE-CS Joint Conference on Digital Libraries*, 2002.

Librarians Association of the University of California. New Horizons in Scholarly Communications. URL: *http://libweb-01.ucsc.edu/scomm/*

Linda L. Hill, James Frew, and Qi Zheng. *Geographic Names - The Implementation of a Gazetteer in a Georeferenced Digital Library. CNRI D-Lib Magazine*, January, 1999.

Linda O'Brien and Peter Sidorko, *Integrating information, education and technology services*, paper presented at Educause 2000, <*http://www.educause.edu/ir/library/pdf/EDU0027.pdf*>.

Lisa Freeman. *Testimony prepared on behalf of the Association of American University Presses for the National Information Infrastructure Task Force Working Group on Intellectual Property*. In *JEP*, 1994.

Lorcan Dempsey. Network resource discovery: a European library perspective. British Library. Research and Development Department, 1994. URL: *http://www.lub.lu.se/UB2proj/LIS_collection/lorcan.html*

Lorna Unwin, Kate Stephens, and Neil Bolton, *The role of the library in distance education*, British Library, 1998.

Luis Gravano, Chen-Chuan K. Chang, Héctor García-Molina, and Andreas Paepcke. *STARTS: Stanford protocol proposal for Internet retrieval and search*. Number SIDL-WP-1996-0043; 1997-68. Stanford University, August, 1996. Accessible at http://dbpubs.stanford.edu/pub/1997-68.

Lynn, M. Stuart. The Relationship Between Digital and Other Media Conversion Processes: A Structured Glossary of Technical Terms. Commission for Preservation and Access. Technology Assessment Advisory Committee. August 1990. (160 K)

M. Baker. Changing Communication Environments in MosquitoNet. In *Proceedings of the IEEE Workshop on Mobile Computing Systems and Applications*, Dec, 1994.

Michael Jensen. *Need-Based Intellectual Property Protection and Networked University Press Publishing*. In *IP Workshop Proceedings*, 1994.

Michael Khoo. Community Design of DLESE's Collections Review Policy: A Technological Frames Analysis. In *Proceedings of the First ACM/IEEE-CS Joint Conference on Digital Libraries*, 2001.

Michael L.W. Jones, Robert H. Rieger, Paul Treadwell, and Geri K. Gay. Live from the Stacks: User Feedback on Mobile Computers and Wireless Tools for Library Patrons. In *Proceedings of the Fifth ACM International Conference on Digital Libraries*, 2000.

Michael Lesk. Image Formats for Preservation and Access. Commission for Preservation and Access. Technology Assessment Advisory Committee. July 1990. URL: *http://www.ifla.org/documents/libraries/net/lesk.txt*

Michael R. Genesereth and Steven P. Ketchpel. Software Agent. *Communications of the ACM*, 37(7), July, 1994.

Michael R. Genesereth, Arthur M. Keller, and Oliver M. Duschka. Infomaster: An Information Integration System. In *Proceedings of the International Conference on Management of Data*. ACM Press, Tucson, Ariz. 1997.

Michael Schwartz, ed. Report of the Distributed Indexing/ Searching Workshop. May 28-19, 1996. Cambridge, Massachusetts. Sponsored by the World Wide Web Consortium. URL: *http://www.w3.org/Search/9605-Indexing-Workshop/*

Michelle Baldonado, Chen-Chuan K. Chang, Luis Gravano, and Andreas Paepcke. *Metadata for Digital Libraries: Architecture and Design Rationale*. Number SIDL-WP-1997-0055; 1997-26. Stanford University, 1997. Accessible at http://dbpubs.stanford.edu/pub/1997-26.

Michelle Baldonado, Chen-Chuan K. Chang, Luis Gravano, and Andreas Paepcke. *Metadata for Digital Libraries: Architecture and Design Rationale*. In *Proceedings of the Second ACM International Conference on Digital Libraries*, pp. 47-56, 1997. At http://dbpubs.stanford.edu/pub/1997-26.

Miriam Bonham. Library services through electronic mail. College & Research Libraries News, 48(9), 537-538. October 1987.

Mitchell N. Charity. *Multiple Standards? No problem.* In *Proceedings of the First Annual Conference on the Theory and Practice of Digital Libraries*, 1994.

MJ Antonelli, et al. The University of North Texas Libraries' online reference help desk. In: Digital reference service in the new millennium. Neal-Schuman Publishers, 2000.

Mohamed Kholief, Kurt Maly, and Stewart Shen. Event-Based Retrieval from a Digital Library containing Medical Streams [short paper]. In *Proceedings of the Third ACM/IEEE-CS Joint Conference on Digital Libraries*, 2003.

Moises Goldszmidt and Mehran Sahami. *A Probabilistic Approach to Full-Text Document Clustering.* SRI International, 1998.

Mushirul Hasan (ed), Knowledge, Power and Politics: Educational Institutions in India, Roli Books (New Delhi, 1998)

N. Asokan, P.A. Janson, M. Steiner, and M. Waidner. The state of the art in electronic payment systems. *Computer*, 30(9):28-35, September, 1997.

N. Gershon, W. Ruh, J. LeVasseur, J. Winstead, and A. Kleiboemer. Searching and Discovery of Resources in Digital Libraries. In *Advances in Digital Libraries '95*, 1995.

N.J. Belkin and W. Bruce Croft. Information filtering and information retrieval: two sides of same coin? *Communications of the ACM*, 35(12):29-38, December, 1992.

Nancy A. Van House, Mark H. Butler, Virginia Ogle, and Lisa Schiff. *User-Centered Iterative Design for Digital Libraries: The Cypress Experience. D-Lib Magazine*, Feb, 1996.

Nancy A. Van House. *User Needs Assessment and Evaluation for the UC Berkeley Electronic Environmental Library Project.* In *Proceedings of the Second Annual Conference on the Theory and Practice of Digital Libraries*, 1995.

National Digital Library Federation (NDLF). America's Heritage: Mission and Goals for a National Digital Library Federation. URL: *http://www.ifla.org/documents/libraries/net/digfed2.htm*

Neil Daswani, Dan Boneh, Hector Garcia-Molina, Steven Ketchpel, and Andreas Paepcke. *A Generalized Digital Wallet Architecture.* In *Proceedings of the 3rd USENIX Workshop on Electronic Commerce, p. 121-39*, 1998.

Newby, Gregory B. The Digital Electronic Library. January 29, 1991. URL: *http://www.ifla.org/documents/libraries/net/newby.txt*

Nick Craswell and Peter Bailey. Server Selection on the World Wide Web. In *Proceedings of the Fifth ACM International Conference on Digital Libraries*, 2000.

OCLC Research Libraries Advisory Committee. URL: *http://www.oclc.org/oclc/man/9680rldc/toc.htm*

OCLC. Tomorrow's Access, Today's Decisions: Ensuring Access to Today's Electronic Resources Tomorrow. Proceedings of the Fourteenth Annual Conference of Research Library Directors. Sponsored by OCLC and the OCLC Research Libraries Advisory Committee. URL: *http://www.oclc.org/oclc/man/9680rldc/toc.htm*

Philip G. Altbach and Patti McGill Peterson, (eds) Higher Education in the 21st Century: Global Challenge and National Response Institute of International Education/ Boston College Center for International Higher Education (New York, 1999)

Richard Biddiscombe, "The changing role of the information professional in support of learning and research," in: Frederick C. Lynden and Elizabeth A. Chapman (eds.), *Advances in librarianship*, 23, 2000.

Richard Giordano. Digital Libraries and Impacts on Scientific Careers. In *Proceedings of DL'96*, 1996.

Robert E. Kent and Christian Neuss. Creating a web analysis

and visualization environment. In *Proceedings of the Second International World-Wide Web Conference*, 1994.

Robert J. Hall. *Agents Helping Agents: Issues in Sharing How-to Knowledge*. In *AAAI Spring Symposium on Information Gathering*, 1995.

Robert Johansen. *Teleconferencing and beyond : communications in the office of the future*. McGraw-Hill data communications book series. McGraw-Hill, 1984.

Sheila Webber and Bill Johnston, "Conceptions of information literacy: new perspective and implications," *Journal of Information Science*, 26(6), 2000.

Suma Chitnis and Philip G. Altbach, (eds) Higher Education Reform in India: Experiences and Perspectives, Sage Publications (New Delhi, 1993)

William P. Birmingham, Edmund H. Durfee, Tracy Mullen, and Michael P. Wellman. The Distributed Agent Architecture of the University of Michigan Digital Library (Extended Abstract). In *AAAI Spring Symposium on Information Gathering*, 1995. .

Wilma Alexander, "Adaptive developments for learning in the hybrid library," *Ariadne* 24, June 2000, *<http://www.ariadne.ac.uk/issue24/sellic/intro.html>*.

Yi-Chun Chu, David Bainbridge, Matt Jones, and Ian H. Witten. Realistic books: A bizarre homage to an obsolete medium? In *Proceedings of the Fourth ACM/IEEE-CS Joint Conference on Digital Libraries*, 2004.

Glossary

Access management Control of access to material in digital libraries. Sometimes called terms and conditions or rights management.

ACM Digital Library A digital library of the journals and conference proceedings published by the Association for Computing Machinery.

Alexandria Digital Library A digital library of geospatial information, based at the University of California, Santa Barbara.

Aligning Recognizing the relationship between an institution and the external environment, seeking to "match" internal strengths with external opportunities, and thereby heighten the flow of resources to the institution

American Memory and the National Digital Library Program The Library of Congress's digital library of materials converted from its primary source materials related to American history.

Applet A small computer program that can be transmitted from a server to a client computer and executed on the client.

Archival Image An image meant to have lasting utility. Archival images are usually kept off-line on a cheaper storage medium such as CD-ROM or magnetic tape, in a secure environment. Archival images are of a higher resolution and quality than the digital image delivered to the user on-screen. The file format most often associated with archival images is TIFF, or Tagged Image File Format, as compared to on-screen viewing file formats, which are usually JPEGs and GIFs.

Archival Scans Digital images serve as surrogates of the original. At this point in time, there is no such thing as an Archival or Preservation scan that acts as an exact replica or replacement of the original, as it is not yet possible to record every piece of information found in the original with today's scanner technology.

Archives Collections with related systems and services, organized to emphasize the long-term preservation of information.

ARPA (DARPA) The Defecse Advanced Research Projects Agency (DARPA) is the central research and development organization for the Department of Defense (DoD). It manages and directs selected basic and applied research and development projects for DoD, and pursues research and technology where risk and payoff are both very high and where success may provide dramatic advances for traditional military roles and missions and dual-use application.

Art and Architecture Thesaurus A controlled vocabulary for fine art, architecture, decorative art, and material culture, a project of the J. Paul Getty Trust.

Artifacts Visual digital effects introduced into an image during scanning that do not correspond to the original image being scanned. Artifacts might include pixellation, dotted or straight lines, regularly repeated patterns, moire, etc.

ASCII (American Standard Code for Information Interchange) (ISO 641) The most widely used character set encoding. 7 bits per character; limited to 128 mainly English-language characters.

Authentication Validation of a user, a computer, or some digital object to ensure that it is what is claims to be.

Authorization Giving permission to a user or client computer to access specific information and carry out approved actions.

Automatic indexing Creation of catalog or indexing records using computer programs, not human cataloguers.

AVI: Audio-Video Interleaved (".avi") ideo for Windows file format.

Boolean searching Methods of information retrieval where a query consists of a sequence of search terms, combined with operators, such as "and", "or", and "not".

Brand or brand promise A warrant, a trustmark, a promise that an organization makes to its internal stakeholders and external customers. Brands exist only in the minds of people. A successful brand is perceived by your most important external audiences as the only solution to a problem they have. Internal audiences must perceive the brand promise as worthy of their commitment. As such, all audiences must perceive a brand to be important, believable, and unique

Broad System of Ordering (BSO) A general subject classification scheme, commissioned by UNESCO, intended to be a switching language among existing classification schemes and thesauri to make them mutually compatible on a general level. It provides about 4,000 subdivisions.

Browser A general-purpose user interface, used with the Web and other online information services. Also known as a Web browser.

Browsing Exploration of a body of information, based on the organization of the collections or scanning lists, rather than by direct searching.

Cache A temporary store that is used to keep a readily available copy of recently used data or any data that is expected to be used frequently.

California Digital Library A digital library that serves the nine campuses of the University of California.

Cascading Style Sheets A new approach to increasing control over the visual formatting of HTML documents (e.g. spacing, colours, backgrounds, choice of fonts, drop shadows, layering, relative and absolute positioning, on/off visibility of options, choice of media such as print, display, braille, aural). CSS tags are in a separate document or part of the document (rather than being embedded in the text as with traditional HTML), so can be changed, updated across multiple documents quickly. Cascading style sheets can be cached locally and reused, so their deployment can result in bandwidth/response time gains.

Catalog A collection of bibliographic records created according to an established set of rules.

CCD Array Charge-Coupled Device array. Light sensitive diodes used in scanners and digital cameras that sweep across an image during capture and, when exposed to light, generate a series of digital signals that are converted into pixel values.

CCITT Group 4 Fax CCITT have developed a series of compression mechanisms for transmitting black and white images across telephone lines by fax machines. The standards are officially known as CCITT Recommendations T.4 and T.6 but are more commonly known as Group 3 and Group 4 compression respectively. Group 4 Fax is in common use.

CD-DA: Compact Disc-Digital Audio, or CD-Audio 1980 standard known as Red Book that defined music compact discs in terms sampling rate (44,100 samples per second), range of values (65,536), and physical format: lead in (contains table of contents and each track's location), program area (tracks) and lead out (silence).

CD-i Compact Disc Interactive Green Book standard, based on Yellow Book Mode 2 that defines the disc, its contents, special compression methods for audio and visual data, an interleaving method for audio, video and textual data, and a hardware and software system designed to interact with television and stereo systems and, more recently, with the Web.

CD-R Compact Disc-Recordable Orange Book, Part II, 1988 specification that supports one-time recording onto disc of all types of random access data, using a laser-sensitive dye layer in the disc make-up.

CD-ROM: Compact Disc-Read Only Memory 1983 Yellow Book standard retained the physical format of Red Book, added more error correction, and allowed two data structures: Mode 1 (ISO 9660), best for data unforgiving of error such as computer programs or databases; and Mode 2, for data more tolerant of error such as audio, video and graphics.

CD-RW Compact Disc-Rewritable Orange Book, Part III, 1994 supports erasable disc recording based on a phase-change- sensitive film in the disc make-up. Not backward compatible with CD players or CD-ROM drives due to a difference in media reflectivity.

CGI (Common Gateway Interface) A programming interface that enables a Web browser to be an interface to information services other than Web sites.

CGM Computer Graphics Metafile Standard for the storage and exchange of 2D graphical data. Initially was a vector format, but has recently been extended to include Raster storage capabilities. Four international standardized profiles have been developed which specify how CGM will be used in within MIME-compliant e-mail and on the Web.

Chemical Abstracts A secondary information service for chemistry.

Classification An organization of library materials by a hierarchy of subject categories.

Client A computer that acts on behalf of a user, including a user's personal computer, or another computer that appears to a server to have that function.

CNI (Coalition for Networked Information) A partnership of the Association for Research Libraries and Educause to collaborate on academic networked information.

Collection Interface Agent A program which interacts with the Collection Registry. For searchable collections (Z39.50, FTL, ...) it takes care of talking to the remote collection, submitting searches, fetching and processing results. It is also referred to as a CIA or a collection agent.

Collection Registry The database in which descriptions of collections are stored.

Communication The creation of customized and segmented messages founded on careful listening that address both institution and audience needs and goals

Competitive positioning Developing and communicating powerful and meaningful differences between your offerings and those of your competition

Complex object Library object that is made up from many inter-related elements or digital objects.

Compression Reduction in the size of digital materials by removing redundancy or by approximation; lossless compression can be reversed; lossy compression can not be reversed since information is lost by approximation.

Compression/Decompression The reduction of image file size for processing, storage, and transmission. The quality of the image may be affected by the compression techniques used and the level of compression applied. Decompression is the process of retrieving compressed data and reassembling it so that it resembles its original form before compression. There are two types of compression:

Lossless compression is a process that reduces the storage space needed for an image file without loss of data. If an image has undergone lossless compression, it will be identical to the image before it was compressed. Primarily used with bitonal images.

Lossy compression is another process that reduces the storage space needed for an image file, but it discards information (information that is "redundant" and not perceptible to the human eye). If an image that has undergone lossy compression is decompressed, it will differ form the image before it was compressed, even though the difference may be difficult for the human eye to detect.

Computational linguistics The branch of natural language processing that deals with grammar and linguistics.

Concept Space Graph of terms occurring within objects linked to each other by the frequency with which they occur together.

Connversion Transformation of information from one medium to another, including from paper to digital form.

Controlled vocabulary A set of subject terms, and rules for their use in assigning terms to materials for indexing and retrieval.

Coordinating/steering committee The administrative and faculty leaders who oversee the strategic planning process. Members of the coordinating/steering committee typically also serve as either chairs or members of the essential task area committees

CORBA A standard for distributed computing where an object on one computer invokes an Object Request Broker (ORB) to interact with an object on another computer.

CORE A project from 1991 to 1995 by Bellcore, Cornell University, OCLC, and the American Chemical Society to convert chemistry journals to digital form.

Core values Enduring beliefs which institution—and the

people who inhabit it—hold in common and endeavor to put into action. Core values guide your institution's faculty, staff, administrators and, to some degree, students, in performing their work. Core values can be relatively informal yet still enduring. Values lead individuals within organizations to believe that some goals or ends are legitimate or correct and other goals are illegitimate or wrong. Core values are often expressed in a statement of values

Corporation for National Research Initiatives (CNRI) A non-profit organization dedicated to formulating, planning, and carrying out national-level research initiatives on the use of network-based information technology. CNRI is concentrating on research and development for the National Information Infrastructure, working collaboratively with industry, academia, and government.

Cryptolope Secure container used to buy and sell content securely over the Internet, developed by IBM.

CSS (Cascading Style Sheets) System of style sheets for use with HTML, the basis of XLS.

CSTR (Computer Science Technical Reports project) A DARPA-funded research project with CNRI and five universities, from 1992 to 1996.

Customers Any person who brings dollars or other valued resources into the organization. Customers include prospective students, current students, donors, and alumni

DARPA (Defense Advanced Research Projects Agency) A major sponsor of computer science research in the U.S., including digital libraries. Formerly ARPA.

Data type Structural metadata associated with digital data that indicates the digital format or the application used to process the data.

Derived Data Data that was originally supplied in one form, but was converted to another form using some automated process.

Derived Image (Derivative Image) An image that has been created from another image through some kind of automated process, usually involving a loss of information. Techniques used to create derived images include sampling to a lower resolution, using lossy compression techniques, or altering an image using image processing techniques.

DES (Data Encryption Standard) A method for private key encryption.

Desktop metaphor User interface concept on personal computers that represents information as files and folders on a desktop.

Dewey Decimal Classification A classification scheme for library materials which uses a numeric code to indicate subject areas.

DHTML: Dynamic HTML Denotes recent developments by both Netscape and Microsoft that use a combination of Cascading Style Sheets (see below) and a scripting language such as Visual Basic script or Javascript to merge the HTML document with the style sheet. Supports greater creative control over the visual presentation of an HTML page and allows the page to respond dynamically without a call to the server, to user-generated events.

DID Document Image Decoding, a methodology for document recognition founded on statistical communication theory.

Dienst An architecture for digital library services and an open protocol that provides those services, developed at Cornell University, used in NCSTRL.

Digital archeology The process of retrieving information from damaged, fragmentary, and archaic data sources.

Digital Camera Copystand scanners that resemble microfilming stands. The digital camera directly captures an image without the use of film. Source material is placed on the stand and the camera is moved up or down in order to fit the material into its field of view, which allows for the scanning of a range of differently-sized materials. Resolution of digital cameras is usually fixed and is expressed as a pixel ratio.

Digital Image An electronic photograph scanned from an original document, made up of a set of picture elements ("pixels"). Each pixel is assigned a tonal value (black, white, a shade of gray, or color) and is represented digitally in binary code (zeros and ones). The term "image" does not imply solely visual materials as source material; rather, a digital image is simply a representation of whatever is being scanned, whether it be manuscripts, text, photographs, maps, drawings, blueprints, halftones, musical scores, 3-D objects, etc.

Digital Libraries Digital libraries basically store materials in electronic format and manipulate large collections of those materials effectively.

Digital Libraries Initiative A digital libraries research program. In Phase 1, from 1994 to 1998, NSF/DARPA/NASA funded six university projects

Digital Library Definitions of the digital library range from narrow to broad, with some disagreement on the actual function of a digital library. Clifford Lynch defines the digital library as "an electronic information access system that offers the user a coherent view of an organized, selected, and managed body of information." This definition recognizes the more traditional role of a library in the digital world: at the very least, a digital library should offer services along with information, such as indexing or cataloging. Users of digital library resources may come to expect (and already do expect) more sophisticated fuctions, such as information and knowledge management services, resource discovery mechanisms, and personalization of access and monitoring of new and existing digital resources. In his paper, "What is a Digital Library? Definition, Content and Issues," Harter discusses the properties of a digital library in terms of several categories on a scale from the narrow view to the broad. Some of the concepts he considers include: types of information resources: selection, organization, and authority control of information resources; authorship; physical and logical location of resources; access to resources; who are the defined user groups; and what services are offered and by whom (or what)? The Task Force on Archiving Digital Information makes a further distinction between digital libraries and digital archives. The Task Force defines digital archives as "repositories of digital information that are collectively responsible for ensuring, through exercising various migration strategies, the integrity and long-term accessibility of the nation's social, economic, cultural, and intellectual heritage instantiated in digital form." Digital libraries, on the other hand, collect and provide access to digital information, but they may or may not provide long-term storage and access to that information.

Digital Library Federation The Federation is comprised of leaders of fifteen of the nation's largest research libraries and archives and the Commission on Preservation and Access (*CPA*). A primary goal of the Federation is the implementation of a distributed, open digital library accessible across the global Internet. The library will consist of collections expanding over time in number and scope to be created from the conversion of digital form of documents contained in founding member and other libraries and archives, and from the incorporation of holdings already in electronic form.

Digital object An item as stored in a digital library, consisting of data, metadata, and an identifier.

Digital signature A cryptographic code consisting of a hash, to indicate that data has not changed, that can be decrypted with the public key of the creator of the signature.

Diodes Light-sensitive electronic components used by the scanner during image capture. Diodes sense the presence or absence of light and create a digital signal that the computer then converts into pixel values.

Dissemination The transfer from the stored form of a digital object in a repository to a client.

Distributed computing Computing systems in which services to users are provided by teams of computers collaborating over a network.

DLI Digital Libraries Initiative. Six research projects developing new technologies for digital libraries — storehouses of information available through the Internet, -funded through a joint initiative of the National Science Foundation (NSF), the Department of Defense Advanced Research Projects Agency (ARPA), and the National Aeronautics and Space Administration (NASA). The projects' focus is to dramatically advance the means to collect, store, and organize information in digital forms, and make it available for searching, retrieval, and processing via communication networks — all in user-friendly ways.

D-Lib Magazine A monthly, online publication about digital libraries research and innovation.

DLITE An experimental user interface used with the Stanford University InfoBus.

Document Digital object that is the analog of a physical document, especially textual materials; a document model is an object model for documents.

DOI Digital Object Identifier Being jointly developed by the Association of American Publishers and the Corporation for National Research Initiatives (CNRI) to identify digital objects—which could be books, chapters, articles, images, recordings, videos or other creative works—primarily for the purposes of effective rights management and digital commerce. Not unlike ISBNs in formulation: a component to the left of the slash denotes the registrant's prefix, and the component to the right of the slash is the object's unique identifier, as assigned by the registrant (e.g. 10.65478/45920). Some publishers have begun implementing a DOI prototype.

DOI (Digital Object Identifier) An identifier used by publishers to identify materials published electronically, a form of handle.

Domain name The name of a computer on the Internet; the domain name service (DNS) converts domain names to IP addresses.

Dots per inch (dpi) A measurement of the scanning resolution of an image or the quality of an output device. DPI expresses the number of dots a printer can print per inch, or that a monitor can display, both horizontally and vertically.

Driving forces Factors that impact aninstitution and initiate change. Driving forces can be anticipated and unanticipated, controllable and uncontrollable. They can include a major threat or pressure from the external environment, an emerging opportunity, an internal crisis or setback, or new leadership

DSSSL (Document Style Semantics and Specification Language) A general purpose system of style sheets for SGML.

DTD (Document Type Definition) A mark-up specification for a class of documents, defined within the SGML framework.

DTD Document Type Definition. Documents are regarded as having types, just as other objects processed by computers do. The type of a document is defined by its constituent parts and structure. A DTD defines the structure of an SGML (Standard Generalized Markup Language) document.

Dublin Core (Definition taken from http://www.purl.org/dc). A metadata element set intended to facilitate discovery of electronic resources. Two features of the Dublin Core metadata element set are simplicity and extensibility. Dublin Core is intended to be usable by both non-catalogers and specialists alike, to provide an economic alternative to more elaborate descriptive models such as full MARC cataloging, and be flexible enough to encode the structure and semantics inherent in rich descriptive standards. The Dublin Core seeks to promote a commonly understood set of descriptors to help facilitate interoperability across disciplines. The Dublin Core can be mapped to the MARC record and a variety of output structures can be generated.

DVD Audio, DVD-ROM, DVD-R, DVD-RAM, DVD Video The next-generation optical disc formats, with higher storage capacity (8-15 times more) than its CD equivalents. "DVD" used to stand for Digital Video Disc, then Digital Versatile Disc, now it is just DVD.

Dynamic object Digital object where the dissemination presented to the user depends upon the execution of a computer program, or other external activity.

Dynamic Range (Bit-depth) The number of colors or shades of grey that can be represented by a pixel. The smallest unit of data stored in a computer is called a bit. Dynamic range is a measurement of the number of bits used to represent each pixel in a digital image. 1-bit or bitonal means that a pixel can either be black or white. Bitonal imaging is good for black and white images, such as line drawings and text. However, scanning in grayscale rather than bitonal may produce a better looking image. 8-bit color or 8-bit grayscale means that each pixel can be one of 256 shades of color or one of 256 shades of gray. 24-bit color means that each pixel can be one of 16.8 million colors.

EAD Encoded Archival Description. The EAD is an SGML (Standard Generalized Markup Language) DTD (Document Type Definition) intended to assist in the creation of electronic finding aids. Developed at UC-Berkeley, it is now maintained and supported as a standard by the Library of Congress and sponsored by the Society of American Archivists. The EAD can be used to represent complete archival structures, including hierarchies and associations. The kinds of functionality that EAD affords can also be implemented using Dublin Core, and it is also possible to migrate records from Dublin Core into the EAD format if necessary. More information on EAD is available at *http://www.loc.gov/ead*

Electronic journal A online publication that is organized like a traditional printed journal, either an online version of a printed journal or a journal that has only an online existence.

eLib A British program of innovation, around the theme of electronic publication.

Emulation Replication of a computing system to process programs and data from an early system that is no longer available.

Encryption Techniques for encoding information for privacy or security, so that it appears to be random data; the reverse process, decryption, requires knowledge of a digital key.

Entities and elements In a mark-up language, entities are the basic unit of information, including character entities; elements are strings of entities that form a structural unit.

Environment The larger, external political, economic, social, technological, and educational ecosystem in which the college or university exists.

Environmental scan A process for discovering and documenting facts and trends in the external environment that might impact the institution's future.

ESRI Environmental Systems Research Institute.

Essential task areas A key institutional process or activity. Sometimes called domains.

European Digital Library Consortium (ERCIM) The European Research Consortium for Informatics and Mathematics aims to foster collaborative work within the European research community and to increase cooperation with European industry. Leading research establishments from fourteen European countries are members of ERCIM.

Expression The realization of a work, by expressing the abstract concept as actual words, sounds, images, etc.

Fair use A concept in copyright law that allows limited use of copyright material without requiring permission from the rights holders, e.g., for scholarship or review.

Federated digital library A group of digital libraries that support common standards and services, thus providing interoperability and a coherent service to users.

Federated Repositories Organized collections (heterogeneous databases) located in different places but searched transparently as one database via merging and mapping (federating).

Field, subfield An individual item of information in a structured record, such as a catalog or database record.

Fielded searching Methods for searching textual materials, including catalogs, where search terms are matched against the content of specified fields.

File Size The file size of an image is proportional to its resolution. The higher the resolution, the bigger the file size. File size is different from image size.

Finding aid A textual document that describes holdings of an archive, library, or museum.

Firewall A computer system that screens data passing between network segments, used to provide security for a private network at the point of connection to the Internet.

First sale A concept in copyright law that permits the purchaser of a book or other object to transfer it to somebody else, without requiring permission from the rights holders.

Flatbed Scanner An image capture device much like a photocopier. The object to be scanned is placed face-down on a glass plate. The CCD array passes beneath the glass.

FTAM File Transfer Access Method OSI-based file transfer protocol, which has been largely eclipsed by FTP.

FTP File Transfer Protocol A TCP/IP application protocol used as a means of on-demand transfer of text, non-text (e.g. audio) and software files from one system to another. Anonymous FTP allows user to retrieve selected files from a remote system without authorization.

Full text searching Methods for searching textual materials where the entire text is matched against a query.

Gatherer A program that automatically assembles indexing information from digital library collections.

Gazetteer A database used to translate between different representations of geospatial references, such as place names and geographic coordinates.

Genre The class or category of an object when considered as an intellectual work.

Geospatial information Information that is reference by a geographic location.

GIF: Graphics Interchange Format (".gif") Widely used image format that displays well on most computer systems, but is limited to 256 colours. Uses a lossless compression technique. Results in relatively small files available for immediate display alongside text in Web documents, so commonly used for toolbars, icons and inline images. Can be "interlaced" (whole image displays with sharpening clarity rather than sequential line-by-line clear display). One colour can be transparent (good for floating images/icons on backgrounds). Better than JPEG for sharp line, black-and-white, and gray-scale images.

GILS: Government Information Locator Service Developed in the U.S. and now being adopted in other countries, GILS is a decentralized collection of systems containing databases of GILS records describing location and access information for publicly-available government information resources. Z39.30 is the access mechanism that has been specified for searching these systems, but they can also be searched through the Web. There is a GILS-USMARC mapping, and an SGML profile has been developed for GILS records.

Goal Specific, measurable statements of what will be done to address strategic issues. Using the above example, a strategic goal might be to increase enrollment three percent for each of the next five years

Google A Web search program that ranks Web pages in a list of hits by giving weight to the links that reference a specific page.

Gopher Uses hierarchical menu structures (no hypertext linkages) and a character-based (non-graphical) interface to access multimedia documents. Has been rapidly eclipsed by HTTP/World Wide Web.

Gray Scale A range of shades of gray in an image. Gray scales of scanners are determined by the number of grays, or values between black and white, that they can recognize and reproduce.

Handle A system of globally-unique names for Internet

resources and a computer system for managing them, developed by CNRI; a form of URN.

Harvest A research project that developed an architecture for distributed searching, including protocols and formats.

Hash A short value calculated from digital data that serves to distinguish it from other data.

HighWire Press A publishing venture, from Stanford University Libraries, that provides electronic versions of journals, on behalf of learned and professional societies.

Hit 1. An incoming request to a Web server or other computer system.

2. In information retrieval, a document that is discovered in response to a query.

Home page The introductory page to a collection of information on the Web.

HTML: Hypertext Mark-up Language (".htm" ".html") A reduced tag set version of an SGML DTD that provides a set of platform-independent styles (defined by tags) used to define the components of a Web document. HTML 2.0 is an IETF standard; 3.0 was an IETF draft (which have 6 month lifespans); HTML 3.2 was announced May 1996 to supplant 2.0 as lowest common denominator. Version 3.2 incorporates all of 2.0 and popular features of 3.0 such as tables but not frames. Version 4.0 was released as a draft in July 1997. While HTML tags are primarily structure-related, there are increasingly accepted tags for specifying presentation and layout.

HTTP: Hypertext Transfer Protocol (Version 1.1) Supports the hypertext linkages among multimedia documents that characterize the World Wide Web, a collection of HTTP servers. HTTP 1.1 is twice as fast as the initial version, 1.0.

Hyperlink A network link from one item in a digital library or Web site to another.

ICPSR (International Consortium for Political and Social Science Research) An archive of social science datasets, based at the University of Michigan.

Identifier A string of characters that identifies a specific resource in a digital library or on a network.

IETF Internet Engineering Task Force - an all volunteer organization responsible for publishing RFCs and Internet Standards.

IIPA International Intellectual Property Alliance.

IITA Information Infrastructure Technology and Applications

IITF Information Infrastructure Task Force.

ILL Protocol: ISO 10160 and 10161 OSI-based protocol that specifies rules to permit the automated exchange of ILL messages between diverse ILL systems and supports the management of ILL transactions.

Image A set of attitudes or beliefs that a person or audience holds about a college or university. Institutions have multiple images. For example, older alums often view you differently than younger alumni; faculty with tenure often perceive you differently than faculty without. Importantly, an image is how you are perceived and not necessarily how you are. But because perceptions guide behavior, it is very important that you know how you are perceived by the audiences you value most

Image Capture Using a scanner or other device to create a digital representation or electronic photograph of an image. The scanning process is often labor-intensive and costly, requiring a substantial investment in handling and processing original materials and their surrogate images. The current strategy is to capture an image at the highest resolution appropriate to the original, and store it off-line as an archival image on CD-ROM or magnetic tape. Techniques such as lossy compression and subsampling can then be used to create derivative images for use online. In the future, as the ability to deliver high-quality archival scans develops, it will be possible to place the archival scan online without cost of recapture. Scanning can be done in-house or contracted out to a vendor. Whether scanning is done in-house or outsourced, quality of the images can vary widely. Image specifications should be stated clearly in the contract with the vendor and sample images (at varying resolutions) of the materials to be scanned should be requested of the vendor prior to the start of the project.

Image Manipulation or Alteration Making changes (such as tonal adjustments, cropping, moire reduction, etc.) to an image using image processing software.

Image size Describes the actual physical dimensions of an image, not the size it appears on a given display device.

Influencers–People who influence stakeholders or customers. They may also be stakeholders (administrators who influence faculty) or customers (current students who influence prospective students) themselves. Influencers include parents, guidance counselors, club advisors, and others

InfoBus An approach to interoperability that uses proxies as interfaces between existing systems, developed at Stanford University.

information discovery General term covering all strategies and methods of finding information in a digital library.

information retrieval Searching a body of information for objects that match a search query.

Information Visualization A method of presenting data or information in non-traditional, interactive graphical forms. By using 2-D or 3-D color graphics and animation, these visualizations can show the structure of information, allow one to navigate through it, and modify it with graphical interactions.

Informedia A research program and digital library of segments of video, based at Carnegie Mellon University.

Inspec An indexing service for physics, engineering, computer science, and related fields.

Integrated marketing (IM) A listening-first, database-dependent, approach to marketing that includes a willingness to segment and coordinate such strategic assets as product (customer), price (cost), and place (convenience), and to develop effective promotion (communication) strategies for key target audiences.

Integrated marketing communication (IMC) A comprehensive, coordinated, institution-wide effort to communicate mission-critical values and messages in ways that target audiences notice, understand, and respond to. IMC stresses data-driven segmentation, message integration, and evaluation. It includes three critical components: brand marketing, direct marketing, and customer relationship management. The purpose of IMC is to establish the brand, or position, in the mind of a target audience.

Intellectual Property Usage License The authority to employ a partcular intellectual work in a designated way, possibly associated with other specifications of scope.

Intellectual Work The object requiring an intellectual property usage license (i.e., an authored document). This object has an associated individual or agent with authority to grant such licenses.

Internet An international network, consisting of independently managed networks using the TCP/IP protocols and a shared naming system. A successor to the ARPAnet.

Internet RFC series The technical documentation of the Internet, provided by the Internet Engineering Task Force. Internet Drafts are preliminary versions of RFCs.

Interoperability The ability of software and hardware on multiple machines from multiple vendors to communicate.

Interoperability The task of building coherent services for users from components that are technically different and independently managed.

Interspace The Interspace is a vision of what the Internet will become, where users cross-correlate information in multiple ways from multiple sources. It is an applications environment for interconnecting spaces to manipulate information, much as the Internet is a protocol environment for interconnecting networks to transmit data. Navigating information paths and grouping related items is a fundamental operation. So is semantic retrieval and community classification, with interactive support for vocabulary switching across domains and subject indexing for amateur classifiers.

Inverted file A list of the words in a set of documents and their locations within those documents; an inverted list is the list of locations for a given word.

IPv6: Internet Protocol, version 6 (also IPng, "I-Ping", for Internet Protocol, next generation) IPv6 is a new system, currently under development, to be used for assigning Internet Protocol addresses in the future. A consensus of the Internet Engineering Task Force (IETF) has determined that IPv6 will be the next generation system for IP Addressing. IPv6, which is eight sections of 32-bit numbers, will eventually replace the current Internet Protocol addressing scheme, known as IPv4, which is four sections of 8-bit numbers.

IR Information Retrieval

ISBD, AACR2, LC, DDC, LCSH, MARC, etc. Traditional library standards for describing traditional library resources that can be used for electronic resources. Recently-added US MARC tag 856 supports provision of URLs in bibliographic records.

ISBN, ISSN, ISMN Standard bibliographic identifiers for print material that can be applied to electronic books, serials, and music.

ISO 12083 The new international standard for electronic manuscript preparation and markup. ISO 12083 speeds computerized text from author to publisher to typesetter without retyping and transforms the document into a searchable database.

ISO 23950 Secifies the rules and procedures of two systems communicating for the purposes of database searching and information retrieval. There are two parts to the standard: the "origin" portion supports the querying of remote systems; the "target" portion translates queries to the logic of the target database system and returns records or results sets. From a searcher's perspective, the standard enables the searching of different systems through use of one familiar user interface.

ISO Latin 1 (ISO 8859-1:1987 part 1) A common extension of and replacement for ASCII, "Latin 1" is the most commonly used character set of ISO 8859-n (n=1-9), a series of nine 8-bit, 256-character alphabets, for mainly European languages. Used by Windows.

Item A specific piece of material in a digital library; a single instance or copy of a manifestation.

Java A programming language used for writing mobile code, especially for user interfaces, developed by Sun Microsystems.

JAVA Java is a simple, object-oriented, distributed, interpreted, robust, secure, architecture-neutral, portable, high-performance, multithreaded, dynamic, buzzword-compliant, general-purpose programming language.

Java, Active X One use of Sun Microsystem's Java programming language, or Microsoft's Active X, is to support multi-window, multimedia data streaming. Microsoft and Netscape are integrating both technologies into their browsers.

JavaScript A scripting language used to embed executable instructions in a Web page.

JPEG Joint Photographic Experts Group. A compression algorithm for condensing the size of image files. JPEGs are helpful in allowing access to full screen image files on-line because they require less storage and are therefore quicker to download into a web page.

JSTOR A subscription service, initiated by the Andrew W. Mellon Foundation, to convert back runs of important journals and make them available to academic libraries.

Key A digital code used to encrypt or decrypt messages. Private key encryption uses a single, secret key. Dual key (public key) encryption uses two keys of which one is secret and one is public.

LDAPv3: Lightweight Directory Access Protocol, Version 3 A client/server protocol for accessing a directory service, LDAP is a simplified version of the directory access protocol portion of the X.500 protocol designed to run directly over the TCP/IP stack. LDAPv3 is an update developed in the IETF, which addresses the limitations found during deployment of the previous version of LDAP, RFC 1779. It also adds new features, improves compatibility with X.500(1993) and also better specifies how LDAP can be used with non-X.500 and standalone directories.

Legacy system An existing system, usually a computer system, that must be accommodated in building new systems.

Lexicon A linguistic tool with information about the morphological variations and grammatical usage of words.

Lexis A legal information service, a pioneer of full-text information online.

Los Alamos E-Print Archives An open-access site for rapid distribution of research papers in physics and related disciplines.

Machine Learning The ability of a machine to improve its performance based on previous results.

Magic Lenses This is an idea out of *Xerox PARC* where a region of the display (the "lens"), positioned by the mouse, is rendered in a special way. Lenses are specialized local views which might show labels where none were before, or handles on objects, or highlight certain subsets of items.

Mandates Written and unwritten rules that govern and guide an institution and its stakeholders. More formal than values, mandates are sometimes prescriptive in nature and may be directly tied to laws, bylaws, ordinances, articles of incorporation, and charters. Because of their usually more formal nature, mandates are often easier to uncover and delineate than values.–

Manifestation Form given t an expression of a work, e.g., by representing it in digital form.

MARC Machine Readable Cataloging. "The MARC formats are standards for the representation and communication of bibliographic and related information in machine readable form." The MARC formats contain an explicit set of rules for the structure of fields and the content values within those fields. More information about MARC is available at *http://lcweb.loc.gov/marc/*

Marketing action plans Clarification of who will do what and when to achieve the marketing goals

Marketplace A subset of the larger environment in which the college or university must create sustaining exchange relationships with key audiences

Mark-up language Codes embedded in a document that describe its structure and/or its format.

MCF: Meta Content Framework An open format for representing information about content. The content targeted includes web pages, gopher and ftp files, desktop files, email and structured databases. The corresponding meta-content includes indices such as Yahoo!, gopher and ftp directory structures, email headers, data dictionaries, etc. Currently version 0.95.

Medline An indexing service for research in medicine and related fields, provided by the National Library of Medicine.

MELVYL A shared digital library system for academic institutions in California; part of the California Digital Library.

Memex A concept of an online library suggested by Vannevar Bush in 1945.

Mercury An experimental digital library project to mount scientific journals online at Carnegie Mellon University from 1987 to 1993.

MeSH (Medical Subject Headings) A set of subject term and associated thesaurus used to describe medical research, maintained by the National Library of Medicine.

Metadata Term means "data about data", or specifically in the Web context, machine-understandable information to identify, locate, and/or describe Web resources. Equivalent traditional library standards include ISBN and ISSN (identification), shelf mark/call number (location), ISBD and AACR2 (bibliographic description), LC and DDC (subject classification), LCSH (subject headings), and MARC (machine-readable communication format).

Metric A measure of a current state and progress toward a specific goal. Metrics are sometimes called CSIs (critical to success indicators) and KPIs (key performance indicators)

Middleware Software that mediates between an applications program and a network. It manages the interaction between disparate applications across the heterogeneous computing platforms. The Object Request Broker (ORB), software that manages communication between objects, is an example of a middleware program.

Migration Preserving the integrity of digital images by transferring them across hardware and software configurations and across subsequent generations of computer technology. Migration includes refreshment (copying digital files from one media to another) as a means of preservation and access. However, migration differs from refreshment in the sense that it is not always possible to make an exact copy of a database or even an image file as changes in hardware and software occur and still maintain compatibility with the new generation of technology.

MIME: Multi-Purpose Internet Mail Extensions Adds multi-part (e.g. WWW hypertext documents, word processing file attachments, etc.), multi-media (non-text such as audio, graphics) messaging support to SMTP. Also supports message encryption.

Mirror A computer system that contains a duplicate copy of information stored in another system.

Mission statement A declaration of an organization's purpose; its raison d'être

MLaw (".au") Another common Internet audio file format, from Sun Microsystems. Works on all platforms, but of lower quality. Stereophonic.

Mobile code Computer programs or parts of programs that are transmitted across a network and executed by a remote computer.

Morphology Grammatical and other variants of words that are derived from the same root or stem.

Mosaic The first widely-used Web browser, developed at the University of Illinois.

MPEG A family of formats for compressing and storing digitized video and sound.

MPEG: Moving Picture Expert Group (".mpg") A compression standard for video, which transfers all information of every tenth frame, with the subsequent nine frames being transmitted only as significant changes to that reference frame. Works on all platforms, but of lower quality.

MSWord, WordPerfect, etc. (word processing applications) WYSIWYG approach to format coding (coding is hidden). Format coding is proprietary, so can be problems of portability among packages or even between different versions of same package. Commonly used for revisable texts. Can incorporate multimedia file parts.

Multimedia A combination of several media types in a single digital object or collection, e.g., images, audio, video.

Multiple View User Interface Multiple views means that phrases can be drag-and-drop across each individual interface for each information source.

Multivalent Document (MVD) A single document made of multiple layers of difference but intimately related material. Each layer is of homogeneous content, but is of a relatively limited scope and functionality. Layers have dynamically loaded program objects associated with them called behaviors, that manipulate the content, often communicating with other layers and other behaviors to achieve a desired effect.

NASA National Aeronautics and Space Administration. NASA's mission is to advance and communicate scientific knowledge and understanding of the Earth, the solar system, and the universe and use the environment of space for research.

Natural language processing Use of computers to interpret and manipulate words as part of a language.

NCSTRL **(Networked Computer Science Technical Reports Library)** An international distributed library of computer science materials and services, based at Cornell University.

NetBill The NetBill project at CMU's Information Networking Institute is designing the protocols and software to support network-based payment for goods and services delivered over the Internet. NetBill acts as a third party to provide authentication, account management, transaction processing, billing, and reporting services for network-based clients and users.

NetShow Standard Microsoft's competing specification for data streaming. Goes farther than RTSP insofar as attempts to specify a compression and decompression standard in addition to start/stop.

NNTP: Network News Transfer Protocol A TCP/IP protocol that enables newsgroup articles to move smoothly through the Internet. Most newsgroups exist on the USENET network.

Noise Data or unidentifiable marks picked up in the course of scanning or data transfer that do not correspond to the original.

NSF National Science Foundation. An independent agency of the U.S. government with the mission of promoting science and engineering.

NTIA National Telecommunications and Information Administration. Responsible for the Information Superhighway.

Object A technical computing term for an independent piece of computer code with its data. Hence, object-oriented programming, and distributed objects, where objects are connected over a network.

Object model A description of the structural relationships among components of a library object including its metadata.

Objective An activity that will help you accomplish a goal. Objectives, sometimes called tactics, are framed in action plans.

OCLC (Online Computer Library System) An organization that provides, among other services, a bibliographic utility for libraries to share catalog records.

OCR Optical Character Recognition

OLE: Object Linking and Embedding Microsoft's proprietary distributed object system that allows an application to manage part of its contents in another application. For example, an Excel spreadsheet of changing data could be invoked in its up-to-date version from a word processing document.

Ontology An explicit formal specification of how to represent the objects, concepts, and other entities that are assumed to exist in some area of interest and the relationships that hold among them.

OPAC (online public access catalog) An online library catalog used by library patrons.

Open access Resources that are openly available to users with no requirements for authentication or payment.

OpenDoc Aims to enable embedding of features from different application programs into a single working document.

Optical character recognition Automatic conversion of text from a digitized image to computer text.

PAD++ Software which provides a virtual infinite extent, infinitely zoomable work surface, being developed under an ARPA grant at the University of New Mexico. Its multiscale interface, allowing interaction at many scales, is expected to allow the visualization of large scale information structures, and the organization of large and complex work activities. It is integrated with the Tcl/Tk prototyping environment and is being used as the development platform for the University of Michigan's Advanced User Interface (*AUI*).

Page description language A system for encoding documents that precisely describes their appearance when rendered for printing or display.

PageMaker, Ventura, etc. (desktop publishing applications) Proprietary format coding is input as specific commands, and effected only upon output.

PAT Indexing software developed by the OpenText Corp. which serves as the basis for its products used for searching the WWW, intranets, etc.

PDF: Portable Document Format (".pdf") A further development is Adobe's PDF proprietary format, which employs the Acrobat suite of software products to be created, edited, viewed, etc. Is printing device-independent, and supports e-publishing using sophisticated formatting and graphics including embedded links, annotations, thumbnails of pages, and chapter outlines for direct access. Adobe has indicated the intent to incorporate structure as well as layout into PDF by extending it to encompass SGML.

Peer review The procedure by which academic journal articles are reviewed by other researchers before being accepted for publication.

Perseus A digital library of hyperlinked sources in classics and related disciplines, based at Tufts University.

Photo CD PhotoCD is Kodak's proprietary format for the digital storage of high resolution images on CD. The images can be viewed at a range of resolutions and manipulated using image processing software.

PICS: Platform for Internet Content Selection A WC3 (World Wide Web Consortium) working group has proposed a set of metadata labels to support both self-description and third-party description and rating of electronic document/resource content. Goal is to give Internet users the ability to select resources effectively based on that metadata description, which will be carried with resources.

Pixel Often referred to as dot, as in "dots per inch". "Pixel" is short for picture elements, which make up an image, similar to grains in a photograph or dots in a half-tone. Each pixel can represent a number of different shades or colors, depending on how much storage space is allocated for it. Pixels per inch (ppi) is sometimes the preferred term, as it more accurately describes the digital image.

Planning A formalized attitude (and process) that involves selecting a rational course of collective action to achieve a future state of affairs. It includes assessing the present state, setting goals, gathering and analyzing information, evaluating information, developing budgets, making decisions, and acting.

PNG: Portable Network Graphics (".png"; pronounced "ping") Intended to replace GIF, with improvements in error detection and interlacing speed and greater compression rates. An emerging format, but is not yet widely used.

Policy A rule established by the manager of a digital library that specifies which users should be authorized to have what access to which materials.

Port A method used by TCP to specify which program running on a computer should process a message arriving over the Internet.

Portals Windows on a zooming work surface which can be used to bring distant regions close, to give simultaneous views at multiple scales, or, when given special active functionality, to create Magic lenses.

Position Very similar to a brand, a position is where your target audiences place someone in their minds; the words they use to describe when asked.

Positioning The act of building a valued and preferred position in the minds of the target audience. **PostScript** A programming language to create graphical output for printing, used as a page description language.

Precision In information retrieval, the percentage of hits found by a search that satisfy the request that generated the query.

Presentation profile Guidelines associated with a digital object that suggest how it might be presented to a user.

Preservation (As it relates to scanning) Digitizing an original photograph, document, or three-dimensional object is only a method of preservation if the digital file becomes the access tool and the original is no longer available for use. Although high resolution scanning (i.e., scan at the highest resolution possible appropriate to the type of media you are scanning) is recommended for all materials in order to achieve the highest quality possible and to ensure that information held in the original is not lost in the scan. However, the digital file, as of yet, should not serve as a replacement of the original for preservation purposes.

Promotion The downward distribution of messages from a college or university to target audiences that focus almost solely on organizational needs and goals (to contrast, see communication, below)

Protocol A set of rules that describe the sequence of messages sent across a network, specifying both syntax and semantics.

Proxy A computer that acts as a bridge between two computer systems that use different standards, formats, or protocols.

Publish To make information available and distribute it to the public.

PURL: Persistent Uniform Resource Locator An approach to the URL permanence problem proposed by OCLC. A PURL is a public alias for a document. A PURL remains stable, while the document's background URL will change as it is managed (e.g. moved) over time. A PURL is created by a Web administrator who is registered as a PURL "owner" and who maintains a mapping of the

PURL to a current and functioning URL. A PURL is a form of URN.

QTVR: QuickTime Virtual Reality Apple's proprietary product that allows a user to view objects and locations from 360-degrees by accessing a small file and playing it like a QuickTime movie. The user's viewing options (or movement) are actually limited to the number of fixed points from which the real object was still-photographed. Built into Netscape 3.0.

Quality Control Techniques ensuring that high quality is maintained through various stages of a process. For example, quality control during image capture might include comparing the scanned image to the original and then adjusting colors or tonal values, or checking for artifacts.

Query A textual string, possibly structured, that is used in information retrieval, the task being to find objects that match the words in the query.

Query Planning Agent A kind of Task Planning Agent. In many contexts, this means task planners who specialize in query tasks. Some select only from a library of existing plans for executing queries, others construct new plans.

QuickTime Movies (".mov") Apple's proprietary compression standard for video files, now works on other platforms.

Ranked searching Methods of information retrieval that return a list of documents, ranked in order of how well each matches the query.

RDF: Resource Description Framework A technical framework being developed by the W3C to support interoperability of metadata describing any item that can have a URI (see below). Schemes such as PICS and Dublin Core (see below) are standard, predefined vocabularies within the framework. XML is the encoding syntax.

RealAudio A format and protocol for compressing and storing digitized sound, and transmitting it over a network to be played in real time.

RealVideo Progressive Networks' video product that uses stream delivery.

Recall In informational retrieval, the percentage of the items in a body of material which would satisfy a request that are actually found by a search.

Refresh To make an exact copy of data from older media to newer for long-term preservation.

Refreshment The transfer of digital files to a new media on a regular basis. This is the most important part of an institution's long-term commitment to digitization. Technology is usually outdated by the time it hits the marketplace. The data we generate today must be retrievable five, fifty, and a hundred years from now. In order to ensure long-term access to the data, it must be transferred to the most recent and stable type of media storage. In a hundred years, it is very unlikely that any of the computers on our desks today will function. We must make sure that the data can be retrieved by future technology.

Registration The process of adding new descriptions to the registry database.

Registry Database The database in which descriptions of agents (including collections) are stored. Also called the Conspectus database or the registry.

Remora Agents An agent which, given a URL, will check the links of a homepage at a specified interval of time, check a specified homepage for any changes in the homepage at a specified interval and notify the user of any changes, and/or search a specified homepage for key phrases, results of which are emailed to the user.

Render To transform digital information in the form received from a repository into a display on a computer screen, or for other presentation to the user.

Replication Make copies of digital material for backup, performance, reliability, or preservation.

Repository A computer system used to store digital library collections and disseminate them to users.

Resolution The number of pixels (in both height and width) making up an image. The more pixels in an image, the higher the resolution, and the higher the resolution of an image, the greater its clarity and definition (and the larger the file size). Resolution can also refer to the output device, such as a computer monitor or printer, used to display the image. Image file resolution is often expressed as a ratio (such as 640x480 pixels), as is monitor resolution; however, resolution is also expressed in terms of dots per inch (dpi). The asssumed universal monitor resolution for web users is 72 dpi. Image file resolution and output (print or display) resolution combine to influence the clarity of a digital image when it is viewed.

RIFF WAVE (".wav") Originally Microsoft Windows' audio file format, now extended to other platforms. Stereophonic.

RSA encryption A method of dual key (public key) encryption.

RTF: Rich text format A portable output/input format for many word processing packages developed by Microsoft.

RTSP: Real Time Streaming Protocol A proposed industry standard announced by Netscape, Progressive Networks and 40 other companies, this protocol addresses issues like reliability, quality, fidelity, packet loss, and start/stop commands for audio and video real-time data streaming.

Scaffolding This concept is based on the idea that at the beginning of learning, students need a great deal of support, gradually, this support is taken away to allow students to try their independence. Providing support takes place in a number of ways - the way in which the selections are organized in a theme, the amount of prior knowledge activation that is provided, the way in which the literature is read by students, and the types of responses students are encouraged to make.

Scanner A device for capturing a digital image. There are many types of scanners, such as flatbed scanners, drum scanners, slide scanners, and microfilm scanners.

Scanning Method of conversion in which a physical object, e.g., a printed page, is represented by a digital grid of pixels.

Scenario planning The anticipation of and planning for events that might help or harm an organization. For example, a crisis plan is a type of scenario plan that guides an organization in a time of peril

Search term A single term within a query, usually a single word or short phrase.

Secondary information Information sources that describe other (primary) information, e.g., catalogs, indexes, and abstracts; used to find information and manage collections.

Security Techniques and practices that preserve the integrity of computer systems, and digital library services and collections.

Segmentation Dividing large, heterogeneous populations into smaller, homogenous subpopulations and creating, based on research, customized and more desirable products, services, and messages

Semantic Retrieval Searching for words within a concept space (graph of terms occurring within objects linked to each other by the frequency with which they occur together).

Semantic Zooming In a multiscale interface like PAD++, normal, geometric zooming simply changes the size of objects in the view. In semantic zooming, objects change appearance or shape as they change size. For example, a growing dot will become a simple box, then a box with a one-word label, then a box with a longer label, then a rectangle filled with text and pictures. The goal is to give the most meaningful presentation at each size.

Server Any computer on a network, other than a client, that stores collections or provides services.

SGML Standard Generalized Markup Language. An international standard for the definition of device-independent, system-independent methods of representing texts in electronic form. SGML emphasizes descriptive rather than procedural markup. While HTML is a markup language which deals primarily with the appearance of a document, SGML is a more complex system for describing structural divisions in a text (title page, chapter, scene, stanza), typographical elements (changing typefaces), and other textual features (grammatical structure, etc.). The "tags" in SGML preserve the structure of a text, enable the user to constrain searches to particular structural features of the text and aid in the navigation and use of the text. More information on SGML is available at ***http://sunsite.berkeley.edu/SGML/***

ShockWave Macromedia's multimedia product supports games, animated interfaces, interactive ads and demos, and CD-quality audio streaming. Included in Netscape Navigator and Microsoft Explorer.

SICI: Serial Item and Contribution Identifier (ANSI/NISO Z39.56-1996 Vers. 2)

Being developed to identify serial issues and articles uniquely regardless of distribution medium (paper, electronic, microform). Not yet implemented.

Situational analysis A determination of the basic health of the institution and the most important marketing challenges and opportunities facing it. A situational analysis typically involves either a SWOT (strengths, weaknesses, opportunities, and threats) or PO (problems and opportunities) assessment

SMTP: Simple Mail Transfer Protocol A TCP/IP application protocol that is the most widely employed e-mail standard. Does not support transfer of non-text messages or message parts such as images, audio or video, nor word processing or spreadsheet files because their proprietary format coding is non-text. Supports only standard ASCII character set (i.e. no diacritics).

SOIF: Summary Object Interchange Format A structured indexing format that permits structured queries (e.g., matching keywords only against author or title lines in documents). SOIF's support for arbitrary data means it can be used for more complex search applications, such as image and audio searching.

Speech recognition Automatic conversion of spoken words to computer text.

Stakeholders Any person, group, or organization that can place a claim on an organization's attention, direction, or resources. Stakeholders typically include faculty, staff, and administrators

STARTS An experimental protocol for use in distributed searching, which enables a client to combine results from several search engines.

Stemming In informational retrieval, reduction of morphological variants of a word to a common stem.

Stop word A word that is so common that it is ignored in information retrieval. A set of such words is called a stop list.

Strategic issue A problem or opportunity that the college or university wishes to address or take advantage of. Strategic issues typically involve several or all of the 10 essential task areas. For example, a strategic issue might be declining enrollment.

Strategic planning A disciplined effort to produce fundamental decisions and actions that shape and guide what an organization is, what it does, and why it does it.

Strategic planning hierarchy There is a great deal of inconsistency in how the following terms: strategic issue, goal, and objective, are used. With an eye toward establishing a common vocabulary.

Strategy An agreed-upon course of action and direction that helps manage the relationship between an organization and its environment. The goal is to achieve alignment or synergy so that an optimal flow of resources to the institution is achieved.

Structural type Metadata that indicates the structural category of a digital object.

Style sheet A set of rules that specify how mark-up in a document translates into the appearance of the document when rendered.

Subsampling Using an algorithm to derive a lower-resolution image from a higher-resolution image.

Subscription In a digital library, a payment made by a person or an organization for access to specific collections and services, usually for a fixed period, e.g., one year.

Subsequent use Use made of digital materials after they leave the control of a digital library.

Surrogate image A representation of the original image, used for study.

tag A special string of characters embedded in marked-up text to indicate the structure or format.

TCP/IP: Transmission Control Protocol over Internet Protocol Specifically denotes network and transport layer protocols within the Internet 5-layer protocol stack, although is often used to refer to the entire stack. The Internet protocol suite generally corresponds to the datalink, network, transport, presentation and application layers as described above. The Internet non-proprietary suite of protocols allows communications among more hosts and more types of data formats than any other protocol suite.

TEI Headers: Text Encoding Initiative headers Headers for TEI (an SGML DTD) documents, usually scholarly resources such as prose, verse, drama, dictionaries, etc. describing the file (title statement, publication statement, source description), its encoding, its revision history, etc. Becoming more widely implemented.

TEI Text Encoding Initiative. An international project to develop guidelines for the preparation and exchange of electronic texts for scholarly research. The TEI has created a set of SGML DTDs for the encoding of humanities and social science-related texts. More information on TEI is available at *http://etext.virginia.edu/TEI.html*

Telnet A TCP/IP application that allows a remote user to login to applications such as library catalogues. Becoming superseded by Web-based search interfaces that employ a CGI (Common Gateway Interface) program to query a database and return results.

Testbed A platform on which an assortment of experimental tools and products may be deployed and allowed to interact in real-time. Successful tools and products may be identified and developed in an interactive, evolutionary, interdependent process.

TeX A method of encoding text that precisely describes its appearance when printed, especially good for mathematical notation. LaTeX is a version of TeX.

TextTiles TextTiling is a method for partitioning full-length text documents into coherent multi-paragraph units.

Thesaurus A controlled vocabulary with a syndetic structure within a circumscribed subject field used to organize material or information.

Ticer Summer School A program at Tilburg University to educate experienced librarians about digital libraries.

TIFF: Tagged-Image File Format Stores very large amount of information about an image. Supports different types of compression (lossy and lossless). Widely used, but mostly as an intermediary format between scanners and desk-top publishing programs.

TileBars An interface for document that allows the user to make informed decisions about which documents to view based on the distribution of search terms in the document.

Tipster A DARPA program of research to improve the quality of text processing methods, including information retrieval.

Transliteration A systematic way to convert characters in one alphabet or phonetic sounds into another alphabet.

TREC (Text Retrieval Conferences) Annual conferences in which methods of text processing are evaluated against standard collections and tasks.

truncation Use of the first few letters of a word as a search term in information retrieval.

Tulip An experiment in which Elsevier Science scanned material science journals and a group of universities mounted them on local computers.

UDP An Internet protocol which transmits data packets without error checking.

Unicode A 16-bit code to represent the characters used in most of the world's scripts. UTF-8 is an alternative encoding in which one or more 8-bit bytes represents each Unicode character.

Uniform Resource Citation A collection of attribute/values about an object. Some of the values may be URIs. URCs are not formally defined, yet.

Union catalog A single catalog that contains records about materials in several collections or libraries.

URC: Uniform Resource Citation, or Uniform Resource Characteristics Developed in conjunction with URNs as a means of describing Internet-accessible resources.

URCs are a set of values which may include authorship, publisher, datatype, date, copyright status, etc. as well as URIs of various kinds (i.e. its URN, and applicable URLs). The standard also specifies the structure for storing metadata, and the operations for building and querying that structure. It encourages development of URC Subtypes to define data elements appropriate for different types or classes of resources. Not yet implemented.

URI: Uniform Resource Identifier The inclusive term for the set of technologies — currently including URLs, URCs and URNs but extendable — that have been developed under the auspices of the Internet Engineering Task Force (IETF) for naming, addressing, and to some extent describing Web resources.

URL Uniform Resource Locator. A standard addressing scheme used to locate or reference files on the Internet. Used in World Wide Web documents to locate files. A URL gives the type of resource being used and the path to the file. The syntax used is: scheme://host.domain/path filename.

URN: Uniform Resource Name Developed to address the need for a global, persistent, and unique identifier for an electronic resource (as opposed to a URL, which although currently serving an identification function, is tied to the resource's location, which can be multiple and can change at any time). Requires URN registries (to ensure no duplication) and resolution systems (to map to the location(s) of the resource). An example syntax is urn:hdl:cnri.dlib/august95. No implementations to date.

US MARC DTD (see under Metadata-Description) **TEI** (Text Encoding Initiative) - a DTD for a wide range of scholarly resources, initially developed for the humanities.

Vision A realistic, credible, attractive future for your organization. There is no more powerful engine driving an organization toward excellence and long-range success than an attractive, worthwhile, and achievable vision of the future that is widely shared by your internal audiences and most important external audiences.

Vivid descriptors The words or phrases one wishes to establish in the minds of the target audience. Also called brand attributes

Vocabulary Switching The mapping of vocabulary from one discipline onto the vocabulary of another discipline.

VRML: Virtual Reality Modeling Language (".wrl") The current public domain specification (Version 2.0) provides for the design and implementation of a platform-independent, ASCII-based, language for virtual reality scene description. The object must be modeled (i.e. unlike QuickTime VR, it is not a real object that has been photographed). Its appearance will be like computer animation, and is often slow and jerky. Built into Netscape 3.0.

WAIS An early version of Z39.50, used in digital libraries before the Web, now largely obsolete.

Warwick Framework A general model that describes the various parts of a complex object, including the various categories of metadata.

Watermark A code embedded into digital material that can be used to establish ownership, may be visible or invisible to the user.

Web browsers Netscape and Microsoft Internet Explorer are standards for Web browsers, which are software that acts as an interface between the user and the World Wide Web. Browsers are also referred to as web clients because in the client/server model, the browser functions as the client program.

Web crawler A Web indexing program that builds an index by following hyperlinks continuously from Web page to Web page.

Web search engines No standards govern Web search engines. Most are databases of indexed keywords from Web resources, and feature boolean search capability, phrase or word searches, and relevancy ranking. Many provide browsable directory (structured) access in addition to keyword indexing.

Web search services Commercial services that provide searching of the Web, including: Yahoo, Altavista, Excite, Lycos, Infoseek, etc.

Web site A collection of information on the Web; usually stored on a Web server.

Webmaster A person who manages Web sites.

Westlaw A legal information service provided by West Publishing.

WHOIS++ WHOIS++ is another lightweight client/server distributed directory search mechanism that initially had widespread adoption as a means of locating Internet users, but is gradually being replaced by X.500 or LDAP services.

Work The underlying intellectual abstraction behind some material in a digital library.

World Wide Web (Web) An interlinked set of information sources on the Internet, and the technology they use, including HTML, HTTP, URLs, and MIME.

World Wide Web (WWW) An interconnected network of electronic hypermedia documents available on the Internet. WWW documents are marked up in HTML. Cross references or hyperlinks between documents are recorded in the form of URLs.

World Wide Web Consortium (W3C) A international consortium based at M.I.T. that coordinates technical developments of the Web.

X.400: Message Oriented Text Interchange System (ISO 10021/CCITT X.400 1988) Supports encryption, so more secure than SMTP without MIME, and supports non-text message parts. The only protocol from the OSI suite to be currently in common use, mainly in governments.

X.500: CCITT X.500/ISO 9594 Directory Standard An OSI protocol for managing online directories of users or resources which provides a hierarchical structure corresponding to the world's classification system: countries, states, cities, streets, houses, families, etc. The goal is to have a directory that can be used globally. An X.500 directory is distributed in nature (i.e. directory information may be distributed among several open systems) but provides a single view to its users.

Xerox Digital Property Rights Language Syntax and rules for expressing rights, conditions, and fees for digital works.

XLS (eXtensible Style Language) System of style sheets for use with XML, derived from CSS.

XML Extensible Markup Language. Designed to enable the use of SGML on the World Wide Web. XML is a metalanguage (a way to define tag sets) that allows you to design your own customized markup language for many classes of documents. XML is designed for easy and straightforward use of SGML on the web, ease of use in authoring and managing SGML documents, and ease of transmission and sharing of electronic documents across the web. XML is intended to deliver infomration, not just pages. XML preserves the key ideas of SGML, only simplifies them.

Z39.50 The American National Standard Information Retrieval Application Service Definition and Protocol Specification for Open Systems Interconnection. The National Information Standards Institute (NISO), an American National Standards Institute (ANSI) accredited standards developer that serves the library, information, and publishing communities, approved the original standard in 1988 (referred to as Z39.50-1988 or Version 1). NISO published a revised version of the standard in 1992 (Z30.50-1992 or Version 2). ANSI/NISO Z39.50 defines a standard way for two computers to communicate for the purpose of information retrieval. Z39.50 makes it easier to use large information databases by standardizing the procedures and features for searching and retrieving information. Specifically, Z39.50 supports information retrieval in a distributed, client and server environment where a computer operating as a client submits a search request (query) to another computer acting as an information server. Software on the server performs a search on one or more databases and creates a set of records that meet the criteria of the search request as a result. The server returns records from the resulting set to the client for processing. The power of Z39.50 is that it separates the user interface on the client side from the information servers, search engines, and databases. Z39.50 provides a consistent view of information from a wide variety of sources and offers client implementers the capability to integrate information from a range of databases and servers.

Z39.59: ANSI/NISO Common Command Language Standard Prescribes interface commands for standard database search operations.

Zooming Enlarging a portion of a digital image in order to see it more clearly or make it easier to alter.